New Nations and Peoples

Spain

Spain

STEPHEN CLISSOLD

with 35 illustrations and 3 maps

THAMES AND HUDSON · LONDON

© STEPHEN CLISSOLD 1969

PRINTED IN GREAT BRITAIN BY HAZELL WATSON AND
VINEY LTD AYLESBURY, BUCKS

Contents

Note on place-names

Where Spanish place-names have an anglicized version in current use, the latter has been used in the text. Accents have been omitted where this is normal English practice. Both forms (the Spanish in brackets) will be found in the Index; e.g., Castile (Castilla), Leon (León), Catalonia (Cataluña), Saragossa (Zaragoza), etc.

Foreword

'SPAIN,' THE TRAVEL posters assure us, 'is different'. In one sense, the phrase is meaningless; for which country does not differ from its neighbours in its history, national character, culture and institutions? But if some countries may be considered more 'different' than others, Spain is certainly one of them. As soon as we find ourselves south of the Pyrenees, we become aware that, regardless of all regional variations, life takes on a new and distinctive flavour. It is not just a question of bullfights, fiestas, and flamenco singing. At a deeper level of the national temper there are features which set Spain apart.

For the English-speaking world Spain has held a special fascination. George Borrow peddling his Bibles and Richard Ford gathering material for his great Handbook, Washington Irving wandering through the romantic Alhambra or Hemingway gazing upon Death in the Afternoon at the bullring, the soldiers who fought under Wellington and Moore or the volunteers who risked their lives in the Civil War of the nineteen-thirties – all who have in any way found themselves involved in her affairs have felt the power of her spell. Even today, her impact is intense on those who venture outside the cosmopolitan tourist resorts. This may be partly explained by the attraction of opposites; for which peoples could be more dissimilar than the Iberian and the Anglo-Saxon in their origins and ethos? But there is also the fascination of discovering the unexpected correspondences which reveal themselves as one probes more deeply. In the differing patterns of their national destinies, Spain and Britain share at least two great motifs in common. Both stand on the confines of a Europe of which they form a part, but to which they do not feel that they really belong. And each country first won, and later shed, the greatest empire of its time. If it is true of Britain today that she has lost her empire and not yet found a new role, this is a fair description of the condition to which Spain has been subject for the last century and a half.

With the United States, Spain's relationship is different; it is that of ex-empire to modern super-power. What remained of the old Spanish Empire was smashed by Yankee warships in a short, decisive war over Cuba seventy years ago. Today, Spain and the United States are allies. But the overwhelming material superiority of her American ally and the stationing of foreign troops on Spanish soil imply a relationship which is sometimes galling to a nation fiercely independent and still deeply attached to her traditional ways.

At the southernmost tip of Spain, only a few miles of sea separate Europe from Africa. The central feature of Spanish history has been the *Reconquista* or Reconquest – the seven centuries of struggle to roll back the Moslem invasions which first swept up the peninsula from Africa at the beginning of the eighth century. The fanaticism of the Moslem conquerors called forth an answering fanaticism amongst the Christians, who took as their patron saint Santiago Matamoros – St James the Moor-slayer. Catholic, European Spain finally triumphed over Moslem, African Spain, and the élan lasted long enough to win her a great empire in Europe and America and to inspire a golden age of literature and the arts. But what happens to the devotees of the Moor-slayer when there are no Moors left to slay? For a time the Spaniards found substitutes in the Indians of the New World, and in heretics and protestants at home. But as the true sense of national destiny faded, the Spanish fury turned in upon itself, and Christian was set against Christian, Spaniard against Spaniard. The culmination was the Civil War of 1936–9. The scars of this national disaster have now healed, but something of its trauma still remains. After three decades of peace, authoritarian order, and now a rising prosperity, there has come a growing desire for more freedom at home and closer integration with Europe. A country which welcomes seventeen million tourists a year can scarcely remain unaffected by the wider European currents of political and social change, and Spain, like Britain, now stands knocking at the door of the Common Market.

General Franco's régime claims to stand for a reaffirmation of Spain's traditional values, and depicts the rising which brought it to power as a 'Crusade', or a modern version of the Reconquest. But the Reconquest was not just seven centuries of uninterrupted struggle; it comprised long periods when Moors, Jews, and Christians lived together in tolerant coexistence and fruitful cultural interchange. Catholic Spain triumphed not only by force of arms, but by the assimilation of valuable elements from other civilizations. Beneath the surface of the authoritarian Spain of today there slumbers a democratic spirit, a capacity for tolerance and respect for human liberties which are characteristic of the authentic Spanish tradition and which augur well for the Spain of tomorrow. To trace the varied strands which have gone to the making of the rich and complex pattern of Spanish life – the pattern which justifies the claim that 'Spain is different' – has been my aim.

1 The land and the people

STRABO, THE GREEK GEOGRAPHER, compared the peninsula to an outspread ox-hide; indeed, it has not only something of that shape, but the texture too of the creased and crumpled skin of some hoary, earth-encrusted beast. In colour it is for the most part a tawny red, though its northern and western edges are green with our familiar European vegetation. The humid zone stands in sharp contrast to the arid two-thirds of the peninsula. You can fly over the dividing line in a matter of seconds and look down on a bare, empty, austere table-land, higher than any other country in Europe except Switzerland. The northern and central part of this *meseta* or plateau has a hard continental climate – nine months of winter (*invierno*) and three of hell (*infierno*) as the saying is; the southern and eastern part is no less dry, but Mediterranean in character. Spain is not a rich land; such wealth as nature has given her is either hidden in her mines or concentrated in the few well-watered vales such as those around Valencia, Seville and Granada. These fertile *vegas* are lush with every sort of fruit, and in the oasis of Elche, on the east coast, there is even a magnificent grove of palms to affirm the land's kinship with Africa. But, for the most part, the slopes of Mediterranean Spain are given over to the vine and the olive, whilst fields of wheat, poor in yield but still remunerative enough, stretch up to the austere highlands of Castile. In the 15th and 16th centuries a great deal of Spain's wealth – in addition to the gold she got from the New World – came from the herds of sheep which ranged the meseta in their seasonal migrations between winter and summer pasture. Today, though he may not see the animals themselves, the traveller can note their occasional passage from the thick clouds of dust which Don

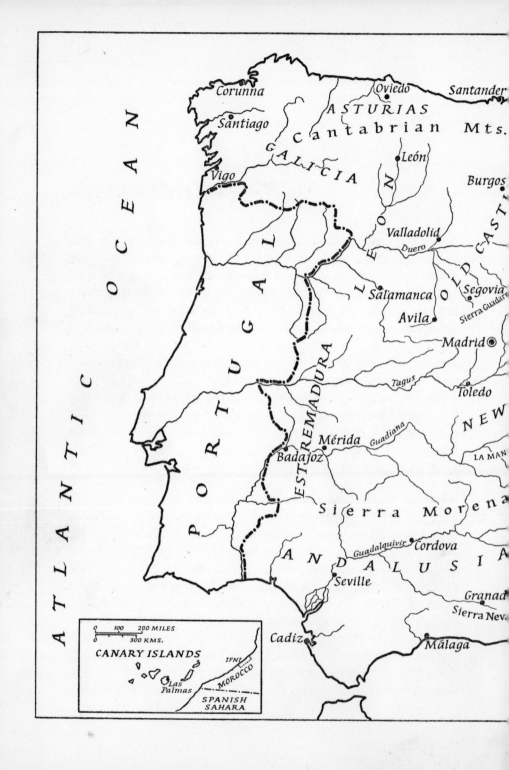

Present-day Spain

Quixote, in his memorable slaughter of the sheep, mistook for the approach of a hostile army.

If you travel overland to Spain, you soon find that the mountains not only rim the meseta, but criss-cross it in a series of irregular ranges through which the train has constantly to tunnel. Nature has partitioned the land into a series of compartments, often differing from each other sharply in climate, custom and ecology. Until improved communications began to break down their isolation, the communities in these compartments led their own lives, developed a keen sense of local patriotism (often centring round the cult of a particular saint) and were suspicious of outsiders and resentful of interference by the central government. Regional diversity has blos-somed in a variegated and picturesque pattern of popular culture. But it has also produced a society where, under stress, separation breeds separatism and individuality leads to anarchy. One region has turned its back upon the rest of the peninsula and looks out upon the Atlantic world as the independent state of Portugal. There have been cases not only of regions but even of parishes declaring themselves independent 'republics'.[1] To hold in check these dispersive tenden-cies, Spain has often needed the rule of a strong, autocratic hand. It is not by chance that the capital, Madrid, stands firmly in the centre of the peninsula and that Castile, the controlling power of the meseta, asserted itself over the periphery. In Spain, good government results from a balance between the centripetal and the centrifugal forces. If the latter become too strong there is likely to be separatism and anarchy; if the former predominate, dictatorship.

GALICIA

Galicia, in the northwest corner of the peninsula, could hardly be more unlike the conventional image of 'sunny Spain'. Its deep, windswept estuaries resemble the fjords of Norway and its green, mist-shrouded hills recall Ireland or Wales. Galicia is, indeed, a Celtic land. The language of its inhabitants is akin to Portuguese, and is so well suited to poetry that, as late as the fifteenth century, Castilian poets would prefer to write their lyrics in Galician, and even in the nineteenth some of the finest lyric poetry of the day was being composed in that tongue. Galicia has never developed a full and distinctive culture of its own, though there has been some movement in this direction in the last two decades. Cultural renaissance is liable to arouse nationalist and separatist sentiment, and fears lest Galicia might gravitate towards neighbouring Portugal may well have been an inhibiting factor. But who, after all, can deny the essential Spanishness of this Celtic land? Galicia contains both the shrine of Spain's patron saint at Santiago de Compostela and the birthplace of her Caudillo, General Franco, at El Ferrol.

Nearly threequarters of Galicia's population of over two and a half million are fishermen and farmers. The pressure of population on the land is greater here than anywhere else in Spain – 98 inhabitants to the square kilometre, as against the national average of 56. Galicia is consequently the classic land of minifundia, or dwarf holdings, and of emigration. In every part of Spain and Latin America one comes across communities of *Gallegos*. Four hundred thousand of them were forced to emigrate between 1910 and 1920, and nearly as many in the following decade. Though the rate slackened in the 'thirties and 'forties, it was up again to nearly a quarter of a million in the 'fifties and is still rising. Behind the neat fields and the deep woods of beech and oak, lie stretches of marsh and moorland which might well be reclaimed if Dutch and Danish experience is any guide, and if the large sums required for this purpose were forthcoming. So far, the Government has preferred to direct its efforts towards stimulating the region's scanty industry, and Vigo and Corunna have been designated amongst Spain's seven 'poles of development'. But the new jobs thus created have not yet gone far towards slowing down Galicia's chronic emigration.

ASTURIAS
Asturias, further to the east, is a land of contrasts. Bare peaks tower above steeply wooded hillsides. Wild, misty valleys shelter farmsteads nestling amongst apple orchards and rich pastures, and the coal mines worked by redoubtable *dinamiteros*, the Asturian miners famed for their toughness and militancy. Oviedo, the ancient capital, is now a modern city thriving from its coal industry, armaments and

chemical plants. Avilés, on the Atlantic sea board, has a gigantic new steel works and a population which has more than doubled in a decade. Yet this go-ahead province is also the most venerable of the Spanish kingdoms. Near the pit-heads round Oviedo stand tiny Visigothic churches built before the coming of the Moslems; under the Picos de Europa, at the magnificently wild eastern end of the Cantabrian Cordillera, the famous cave of Covadonga marks the traditional hide-out of the Christian chieftain Pelayo who repul-sed the Moorish invaders, and thus – so legend has it – set in train the Reconquista.

THE BASQUE PROVINCES

Beyond Asturias lie the city and province of Santander, sometimes known as La Montaña, a northerly extension of Castile spilling over the Cantabrian mountains to provide its only outlet to the coast. Beyond Santander stretch the three Basque provinces of Alava, Viscaya and Guipúzcoa and partly Basque Navarre, the Pyrenean kingdom which passed in the early sixteenth century to Ferdinand of Aragon, widowed husband of Isabel of Castile, on his remarriage to a French princess. To ethnologists and philologists the Basques present an enigma. What is the origin of their race, and how did it come to speak a language quite unrelated to any other in Europe, possibly in the world? There are Basques still living on the French side of the frontier, and at one time the race must have occupied a far greater area than today. According to one theory, indeed, they may have been the original inhabitants of the whole peninsula. Not only their language but many of their institutions and customs are rooted in remote antiquity. The Basques still dance the *jota*, and play *jai alai*, the national sport. They point with pride to the venerable oak tree at Guernica under whose shade the liberties of the Basque provinces used traditionally to be affirmed. Their farms are held on an ancient system of share-cropping, where contracts are often oral and handed down from father to son, or else they are inalienable and held by the whole family, whose head chooses his successor from amongst his sons and relatives. In this way the excessive fragmenta-tion of the land characteristic of Galicia is avoided. With fair soil and rain in plenty, and the right to use communal pastures and forest on the mountain slopes, the Basque peasant gains a tolerable living from his land. He is hard-working, sturdy, pious and intensely conservative.

If the Basques come of the oldest stock in the peninsula, they are also in many ways its most modern and progressive people. They possess a remarkable aptitude for commerce, and their trading and mercantile activities have brought them all manner of international contacts. Like the Scots in Great Britain, whom they resemble in their business acumen and tenacity, they have set the pace for economic development throughout the peninsula. Two of Spain's leading banks are Basque; the construction of the Madrid metro was a Basque enterprise, as is the current programme of expansion in hydro-electric power. Their chief city, Bilbao, is the centre of one of the most heavily industrialized zones in the country. Though its great ship-yards still flourish, the rich veins of iron ore on which local industry has been built are said to be nearing exhaustion. The steel-mills, in spite of injections of United States and German capital, are in need of modernization and cannot produce as cheaply as their European competitors. Whilst attempts are made to keep costs low and to freeze wages, the cost of living continues to rise and social unrest grows. The Basque metal-workers along with the miners of Asturias are amongst the most militant in Spain. Though the authorities continue to keep the situation under control, Basque nationalism is always ready to lend its explosive force to the radical aspirations of the industrial workers. Yet if the energies of this gifted and vigorous people seem often to be at loggerheads with the central authorities it must be remembered that they have given Spain some of her greatest figures such as the soldier-saint Ignatius Loyola, founder of the Jesuits, Unamuno, one of her most powerfully original thinkers, and Pío Baroja, master of the realist novel.

ARAGON
Bordering on Navarre and the Pyrenean frontier stretches Huesca, a large, sparsely populated province sloping down towards the great triangular trough of the Ebro valley which is the heart of Aragon.

Here, in the plain, the Moors have left their mark, both in the *mudéjar* architecture of the capital Saragossa, and in the old irrigation canals, which are the forerunners of the more ambitious works of today. Saragossa is an important manufacturing and administrative centre, the nodal point between the Ebro valley and rail and road communications with Madrid, and also the seat of the famous shrine of the Virgin of the Pillar. The third province of Aragon is Teruel, a stark, thinly populated land of poor soil and small mines of coal, iron, manganese, zinc and sulphur, which commands the passes, bitterly contested during the Civil War, to the central meseta. The Aragonese are noted for their proud independence, their tough-ness, intransigence and their proverbial obstinacy. If Aragon is famous for its fervent devotion to the Virgin of the Pillar, it is also remembered for the great rising of 1933 when the anarchists all but took over the factories and local administration of the entire province. There are no tougher fighters in all Spain than the Ara-gonese. The siege of Numantia, which held out against the Romans until its last defender was slain, and that of Saragossa against Napo-leon's troops, are characteristic of the people's fanatical heroism. Though the marriage of King Ferdinand to Queen Isabel linked Aragon politically to Castile, it had already risen to prominence in the Middle Ages, in association first with Navarre, then with the powerful county of Barcelona. Her soldiers and administrators established Aragonese rule in Sardinia, South Italy, Sicily and still remoter parts of the Mediterranean. The independent Kingdom of Aragon reached this apogee of power in partnership with her neighbours to the East – the enterprising, commercially minded, maritime Catalans.

CATALONIA

Catalonia, which comprises the four provinces of Gerona, Lérida, Barcelona and Tarragona, is one of the most prosperous and densely populated parts of Spain. Gentle valleys lead through vineyards and olive groves to the coast where successive civilizations established their great trading entrepots; the Greeks at Emporion, in the Gulf of Rosas, the Romans at Tarragona, the Catalans at Barcelona. This

Mediterranean land has a more 'European' atmosphere than other parts of Spain, and the transformation of the small ports and pictur esque fishing villages of the Costa Brava into booming holiday resorts has made it known to millions of foreign tourists. Barcelona itself, though it has latterly been slightly outgrown by Madrid, is still the centre of the country's greatest industrial complex. If the Mediter ranean trade was once the source of Catalonia's prosperity, her present wealth was built up on the textile industry. In the economically backward Spain of the nineteenth century, her people showed the requisite adaptability and enterprise, her valleys provided the hyd raulic, and later the hydro electric, power for the mills. They are still a feature of the Catalonian landscape – large, symmetrical buildings, marshalling their rows of working class houses on the banks of the rivers, forming a small scale industry, which was not very efficient perhaps by modern European standards, but capable, behind the shelter of high tariff walls, of laying the foundation for a prosperity which has attracted immigrants from all parts of Spain.

But if economic conditions in Catalonia compare favourably with those elsewhere, her political record has been less happy. The Catalans speak a language of their own derived from Latin, but more akin to Provençal than to Castilian, and possessing a fine medieval and a not inconsiderable modern literature. Their political and administrative institutions evolved under French influence, and their relations with Castile have been subject to constant strain and stress, particularly since the revival of Catalan nationalism in the nineteenth century. The grant of autonomy in 1931, after years of nationalist agitation complicated by social turmoil – for a vigorous anarcho syndicalist movement had taken root in Barcelona – seemed to promise the fulfilment of Catalan aspirations. Then came the Civil War, and – by an ironic twist of fate – that part of Spain which had so often been at odds with its government, now found itself the government's staunchest supporter. The collapse of Repub lican Spain meant the end of Catalan autonomy and the reimposi tion of a revengeful centralism. The passage of time and the return of economic prosperity have done much to heal old scars, but the Catalans have not renounced their dreams of autonomy. The dominance of Madrid is the more irksome in that the Catalans feel themselves, with some justification, to be the more cultured, European and efficient part of Spain.

The Balearics

The Catalans thrive through industry, agriculture and tourism; the two latter activities alone provide the livelihood for most of their cousins in the Balearics. The largest of this group of islands is Majorca. Its agreeable climate, sandy beaches, the beauty of its almond blossom in spring, and of the terraces and steeply wooded slopes of its mountainous north-west coast, now attract a million tourists each year. Here, as on the Costa Brava, the problem is not under- but over-development – the proliferation of villas, hotels and blocks of flats rapidly ringing the whole island. Majorca has long known a moderate prosperity thanks to the fertility of its soil and to its position as an entrepot for trade between Europe and Africa. It reached its heyday between its conquest from the Moors by King Jaime of Aragon in 1230 and its decline which set in at the end of the fifteenth century with the opening up of the new sea routes to America. The nineteenth century saw a revival in the island's trade and the output of her shipyards. Minorca, flatter and less fertile than Majorca, enjoyed its greatest prosperity in the eighteenth century, when the excellent deep-water harbour of Port Mahon served as a base for the British fleet operating in the south-western Mediterranean.

Valencia

Valencia, conquered briefly from the Moors by Castile's hero, the Cid, and incorporated into the domains of Aragon by Jaime the Conqueror in 1238, is also a fertile and prosperous part of Spain. But its fertility is not solely the gift of a bounteous nature, for we are now well into Spain's arid zone, where fertility is the product of centuries of human toil and skill in irrigation. Castellón de la Plana, the most northerly province, is relatively poor and shares the nature of neighbouring Aragon. It is only where the coastal plain broadens out at the approaches to Valencia, third in size of Spanish cities, that we observe the astonishing abundance of this 'Garden of Spain'.

Here careful irrigation can cause the soil to yield as much as four or even five crops a year, and a multitude of tiny holdings, grouped round steep-roofed white-washed *barracas*, support a density of population sometimes surpassing 1,000 to the square mile, amongst the highest in Europe. The secret of all this profusion – the vines, olives, figs, almonds and lemons, the thirty million trees of its great orange plantations, the paddy-fields where enough rice is grown to satisfy half the needs of the whole country – is irrigation. Though it was probably established before their coming, the Moors perfected the system of complex channels and regulated it by a code of usage which is supervised to the present day by the famous Tribunal of the Waters. This still meets every Thursday midday in the porch of Valencia Cathedral, as its predecessor met centuries ago before the mosque which stood on the same site. The Valencians, who speak a dialect akin to Catalan, are a gay as well as a hard-working people, lovers of flowers, fiestas, fireworks, dances and – less predictably, for those who equate Spanish music exclusively with guitars and casta-nets – of brass bands. Yet if we travel on to Alicante, the southern-most province of Valencia, the white cube-shaped houses set amidst the lofty date-palms of Elche give the impression that we are already in Africa.

MURCIA
Murcia also consists of a coastal plain which is fertilized by the irri-gation channels fanning out from the Segura River. Here, too, the land bears an unmistakable African stamp and the magnificent harbour of Cartagena recalls in name at least, if not in the character of the modern town, the ancient Carthage from which its first settlers came. Yet in other parts of Spain Murcia's image is generally not a flattering one. 'Nothing good between earth and sky in Murcia', the saying has it, and army regulations on promotion to the rank of sergeant used to disqualify 'thieves, malefactors, loose-livers and Murcians'. Merely to call someone a *Murciano* is often taken by the Spaniards as abuse. Foreigners have been equally uncomplimentary. Richard Ford declared that 'the better classes vegetate in a monoto-nous unsocial existence', the lower were 'superstitious, litigious and

revengeful', and the roadsides 'studded with crosses, erected over sites where wine and women have led to murder'. Does Murcia truly deserve this ill reputation? Its real crime is surely poverty. For behind the fertile *huerta* rise arid hills which afford only the scantiest of livings to their inhabitants and force many to emigrate. But once rescued from penury and illiteracy, the Murciano can prove his worth like any other Spaniard.

ANDALUSIA

To the south-west of Murcia, flanking the Sierra Nevada which forms the mountainous hinterland of Spain's southern coast, lies the port of Almería and the province of that name – one of the eight comprising what we now call Andalusia. Here, despite the dry, hot climate, and the thinness of much of the soil, nearly one-fifth of Spain's population lives. The heartland of Andalusia is the broad valley of the Guadalquivir, which nourishes the noble cities of Seville and, further inland, Cordova, once the magnificent metro-polis of Moslem Spain. North of this valley rise the bleak and formerly bandit-infested ranges of the Sierra Morena. In places, the bare hills have been gouged and made to yield up the mineral wealth which once won for Andalusia the fame of a rich land, and brought prosperity to the ancient Phoenician ports of Málaga and Cadiz. A variety of mineral deposits are still worth exploiting, most of them on a small scale; only a few, such as the British-owned Río Tinto copper mines, are today of major importance. The sun-drenched valleys need only the magic touch of water to burst into marvellous fertility. Olives, citrus fruits, almonds, figs and vines – for this is the famous sherry country of Jerez de la Frontera – all are found here in abundance and breath-taking beauty. This is the heart of al-Andalus, cultivated by centuries of Moorish skill and industry, whilst the Christian armies closed in on their last small Kingdom of Granada and finally planted their banners over the minarets and battlements of the Alhambra. This is Moorish Spain, romantic Spain – Spain of the bullfights and flamenco singing, of languorous serenades and crackling castanets.

It is also the Spain of desperate poverty, rural de-population, and clamant social injustice. Since the days of the Romans, Andalusia has been a country of great estates or *latifundia*. The Christian kings who ousted the Moorish landowners gave the conquered land to the Church, the military orders, or to individual nobles. In the nineteenth century the extensive church lands were sold to a new class of landowner. But whether the owner was parvenu or aristocrat, the estates needed to be worked and labour continued to be drawn mainly from the pools of landless *braceros* living in *pueblos*. These pueblos were towns in respect of size, but no more than villages to judge from their appalling lack of sanitation, lighting and other services and the absence of all amenities or alternative sources of employment. The wretched pay and the miserable conditions under which the braceros work have long been notorious. Moreover, since they are hired on a seasonal basis, the men are unemployed for much of the year and subsist between jobs on a hand-to-mouth basis. As the landowner seldom visits his property and leaves supervision to a tenant or overseer, he has little personal contact with this shifting labour force and an atmosphere of resentment and fear inevitably builds up which the well-armed *guardia civil* may hold in check but are hardly likely to dispel. Small wonder that anarchism found so many adherents amongst the desperate braceros before the Civil War. Now that the forces of repression are efficiently organized and the more fortunate parts of Spain need labour for their industrial expansion, emigration offers a better safety-valve for discontent. The half-deserted or totally abandoned village is today a harsh note in the smiling but tragic landscape of Andalusia.

ESTREMADURA

Stretching northwards beyond the Sierra Morena up the long frontier with Portugal lies the desolate plateau of Estremadura. It is a monotonous, empty land of big estates, given over for the most part to scrub, heather and gum-cistus, dotted with cork trees and with clumps of ilex whose acorns fatten herds of pigs. Sheep graze on rolling hillsides sloping away towards the Atlantic, the green winter pastures which are the goal of their long seasonal migrations.

Christians battled with Moors over these uplands during the centuries of the Reconquista and then bore their triumphant banners on
to the conquest of the fabulous New World. Here Cortés left his
manor house to conquer Mexico and Pizarro his pigs to conquer
Peru. Estremadura, more than any other part of Spain, is the classic
land of the conquistadores, and its sons who venerated – as she is still
venerated today – Our Lady of Guadalupe carried the cult of their
madonna to the innumerable Guadalupes of America. Where the
Tagus and Guadiana rivers smooth a way through the hill country,
the soil can be made to yield a tolerable harvest; the corn-fields round
Augusta Emerita, the Mérida of today, supported one of the largest
Roman settlements in Spain. Now modern techniques of dam construction and irrigation engineering are transforming this derelict
landscape. In the Guadiana valley, between Mérida and Badajoz,
the construction of the gigantic Cíjara dam has made possible the
intensive cultivation of 300,000 hectares of hitherto semi-barren land
and led to the settlement of some sixty thousand peasant families and
the founding of more than three dozen new towns and villages. Here,
at least, a new chapter is opening for one of the most backward regions
of Spain.

LEON

Leon now consists of five provinces comprising a large and roughly
rectangular tract of territory between Estremadura in the south and
Asturias in the north. It is in general a poor and thinly populated
land, though some of the cities which gave their names to the provinces have been famous in their day: Salamanca, with its glowing
honey-coloured buildings, the seat of one of the most celebrated universities in Europe; Valladolid, once the residence of kings and site
of the country's greatest annual fairs; Leon, the headquarters of a
Roman legion and an 'imperial' city when Castile was but the fief
of an upstart count. Geographically, Leon is a transitional region
between the Cantabrian Mountains and the meseta, and its character
and historical development can best be further considered within the
framework of Castile.

CASTILE

We have now considered the regions – many of them of strongly marked originality – which make up the periphery of Spain; it is time to turn to the rugged core of the peninsula, the heartland of Castile. The name is well chosen, for not only does the central plateau form a sort of geological castle or fortress, but the historic kingdom itself came to birth and grew as the line of castles was gradually pushed south against the Moors. There is an Old Castile and a New Castile corresponding to successive phases of the Reconquista and to differing types of climate. Old Castile, which absorbed Leon, as Leon had absorbed Asturias, is a high tableland centring round Burgos, centre of the medieval wool-trade. It has a harsh, dry climate, and thin though not infertile soil. New Castile, milder in climate, was added after the capture of Toledo, in the geographical centre of the peninsula, towards the end of the eleventh century, but comprised large tracts of land which were mostly uninhabited either as a result of incessant warfare or because of the mountainous nature of the terrain. New Castile is screened from Old Castile by the oblique chain of the Guadarrama which forms a line of natural defences, savagely contested in the 1936–39 Civil War, for the modern capital, Madrid. To the south are the treeless plains of La Mancha, ranged by the immortal knight-errant Don Quixote. These are scorched and waterless lands. Castile's two great rivers, the Duero and the Tagus, flow on through Portugal to the Atlantic, but their gradients are too steep and their flow of water, eagerly syphoned off for irrigation, is too uncertain for purposes of navigation, though it is now being turned to some account for hydro-electric power.

This bare, hard landscape gives an impression of often forlorn emptiness, as if the tired heart of the peninsula had been drained of its life-blood. Dense forest has given place to eroded hillside. The multitudes of transhumant sheep which once gave Spain the wealth of her wool-trade have dwindled to an occasional flock. Even the famous cities of Castile have become museum-pieces; walled Avila, the city of Saint Teresa; Segovia with its Roman aqueduct and fairy castle; the church towers and palaces of Toledo rising above the Tagus gorge as in El Greco's dramatic canvas. The smaller pueblos, slumbering in the dusty midday heat, seem totally bereft of life unless evoked with gentle melancholy in the pages of the essayist Azorín. This is the tragic, noble landscape described so compassionately in the poems of Antonio Machado:

'Wretched Castile, the lord of yesteryear,
Draped in her rags, and scorning everything she does not know.'

Spain's greatness was built on the resources, material and human, of Castile. When these began to fail, national decline set in. 'Castile made Spain', wrote Ortega y Gasset in his celebrated analysis of the national problem, *Invertebrate Spain,* 'and Castile was Spain's undoing'.

The Castilian character is thus central to any understanding of Spain, past or present. 'The Castilian is a good man and true', wrote Richard Ford more than a century ago. 'His manner is serious and marked by the most practical equality; for all feel equal to the proudest noble through the common birthright of being Castilian ... The Castilians, from their male and trustworthy character, constitute the virility, vitality and heart of the nation'. It is a character attuned to their noble and sometimes sombre landscape; tenacious, stoically indifferent to pain, whether suffering it themselves or inflicting it on others. Hence the Spaniard's heroism; hence too his reputed cruelty. Above all, he is an incorrigible individualist. Ganivet, in his famous *Idearium Español,* remarked that each of his countrymen would like to have in his possession a licence inscribed with the formula; 'This Spaniard is authorized to do just whatever he pleases'. Sometimes this extreme individualism leads to arrogance, touchiness and the characteristically Spanish preoccupation with 'honour'. More often it results simply in an innate inability to see another man's point of view, let alone make concessions to it. The word *compromiso* exists in his language, but its meaning is more commonly that of engagement or obligation, rather than of compromise. V. S. Pritchett has amusingly described how one can become aware of this trait simply by watching a Spaniard trying to agree on some trifling arrangement with a friend; 'the Spaniard is considering a most difficult notion; the existence of a personality other than his own'.[2]

Just as Castile is a land of brusque contrasts – fierce heat or cold, sharp contours unblurred by gentle half-lights – so the Castilian tends to go readily from one extreme to another; from apathy to bursts of energy, from silence to rhetoric, from fervent Catholicism to rabid anti-clericalism. One should not however conclude that he is a sort of congenital manic-depressive; the very different quality of *mesura* – moderation, sobriety, and prudence – has always been highly regarded, and the Castilians' warrior-hero, the Cid, possessed this quality to a high degree. But beneath the self-control and courteous good sense which characterizes the Castilian's normal conduct, one becomes aware of deep and passionately held convictions which, when crossed, provoke intransigence and fanaticism.

The Castilian thus tends to make a good ruler and administrator but a poor partner. Though in his sense of the dignity and worth of the individual he is the most democratic of men, he lacks the give-and-take required if parliamentary democracy is to work. He lacks too the commercial sense to be found elsewhere in the peninsula, for the *hidalgo*'s distaste for mere money-making dies hard. Yet he has not lost the will to command nor his assumption that Castile is still called upon to play the leading role in the national life. This leads to internal tensions and makes the achievement of any effective national consensus difficult. Ortega y Gasset went so far as to declare that his country had ceased to exist as a real nation and was no more than 'a great cloud of dust which remains in the air after a great nation has galloped away down the road of history'. Spain has certainly suffered fresh calamities since those words were written, but is such pessimism still justified today? There are great reserves of strength in the Spanish character. Certainly there will be no return along the road of Spain's imperial greatness. But if there is dust, there is also movement. And once the dust has settled, we may well see that Spain is indeed still on the move, but that she has simply changed direction.

New Strands in an old Pattern

We have now noted the motifs which regional diversity contributes to the pattern of Spanish life. Though moulded by tradition, it is not a static pattern. One can still find, it is true, remote corners of

Spain where time seems to have stood still since the Middle Ages; but elsewhere, especially in the large cities and the more prosperous areas, there has been a remarkable quickening in the tempo of change. The last decade and a half have witnessed a particularly rapid economic growth, stimulated by the American military and econo-mic aid which started to arrive in the mid 'fifties. Spain, cold-shoul-dered by the democracies since Franco's victory in the Civil War, began to receive a fructifying inflow of foreign capital and free-spending tourists. The restrictions of an autarchic economic policy were lifted and a new team of governmental technocrats began to work out schemes for the liberalization of trade and comprehensive plans of national development. Though underdeveloped in com-parison with the countries of Western Europe, Spain began to make determined efforts to join the ranks of the industrial nations. In five years she increased her industrial production by 73 per cent. Con-sumption of electrical energy, which in the pre-war Spain of 1935 had been only 18 kilowatts annually per head of the population, rose to 135, that of coal from 366 to 533 kilograms, steel from 14 to 75 kilograms. In 1935, only one Spaniard in a thousand owned a car; now the figure has risen to eighteen in every thousand, and a high proportion of these cars are produced in Spanish factories. If this is still a modest achievement by western European standards, it never-theless denotes a considerable rise in prosperity for Spain's middle classes.

Spain is no longer the predominantly agricultural country of half a century ago. In 1900, two-thirds of her active population worked on the land; in 1966, less than one-third. In Catalonia, the proportion is far less; by 1970 it may have fallen to only about 8 per cent. This is a healthy trend, provided that the reduction of the agricultural labour force goes hand in hand with more efficient farming. But in many parts of the country, agriculture stagnates and still employs a far higher proportion of the population at very low levels of productivity. It is from these areas – over-crowded Galicia and the poor hill-country of Castile, Aragon, Murcia and Estremadura, the huge latifundia of Andalusia – that a stream of emigrants has traditionally come. But this flight from the land has now become a stampede. In eighteen out of Spain's fifty provinces, comprising nearly a quarter of her inhabitants and almost 45 per cent of her territory, the population is shrinking year by year. Whole districts are becoming depopulated, and entire villages either deserted or left to a handful of elderly folk. It is a problem for which there are no easy solutions. What economist would agree, in the interests of a more even social and demo-graphic development, that new factories should be planted indiffer-ently over the face of the land rather than concentrated in economi-cally favoured zones already possessing an adequate infra-structure and plentiful supply of skilled labour? In one or two areas, as in the scheme near Badajoz, the Government has managed to arrest and even to reverse the trend of rural depopulation through costly irriga-tion and resettlement works. But throughout the country as a whole, vast tracts of land are sinking deeper into decay as industry booms and the cities grow. Much of Spain seems in danger of turning into a semi-desert surrounding oases of fertile *huerta* and concentrations of industry.

The influx of immigrants creates new problems for the areas which receive them. Their labour is needed, but if they settle in such num-bers will not the new-comers swamp the native population and alter the whole character and distinctive culture of the region? The Cata-lans are asking themselves whether the children of immigrant Mur-cians and Andalusians will really come to feel themselves to be Catalan, and to speak Catalan, or whether they will de-Catalanize their new homeland.[3] The Castilian-speaking, radically-minded industrial towns of the Basque provinces, surrounded by a Basque-speaking conservative and Catholic peasantry, set a disturbing precedent. Spain is by tradition the most Catholic of countries. But once a peasant leaves his village and its customary religious obser-vances and makes his home in a *barraca* or a crowded room in one of the municipal blocks of flats, he is virtually beyond the ministrations of the Church. Today, the alienation of the Spanish urban workers from organized religion is almost complete.

The chief poles of attraction for the hopeful immigrants are the rapidly growing cities of Madrid and Barcelona. The former, with a population of over $2\frac{1}{2}$ millions, is slightly larger than Barcelona, but its recently developed light industries account for only 9 per cent of the country's industrial production compared with Barcelona's 18 per cent. Madrid's large population of officials, petty civil servants, and rentiers give the city the rather self-conscious air of the nation's capital. Barcelona, with its lovingly preserved old buildings and the extravaganzas of its most original architectural genius, Gaudí, and its radiating network of boulevards, has the bustle of a great Mediterranean port, proud alike of its Catalan character and its European connections. But despite their strongly marked individuality, the two cities are now in their different ways too cosmopolitan to rank as 'typically Spanish'. The westerly winds of change blow through their streets too briskly, eddying turbulently round university faculties, more temperately through banks, business houses and smart new stores, and even ruffling the proverbial lethargy of the bureaucratic siesta. No longer is it appropriate to wish someone long life by the saying 'May death come to you from Spain!' The *sereno* still parades the street at night-time with his stick and his bunch of keys to answer the late-comer's summons and let him into his own home. But those who prefer to spend the evening in front of their television set are at least as likely to watch a football match as a bull-fight, and to listen to pop in preference to *canto hondo*. Spain may still be 'different'; but in the big cities at least we find more and more echoes of our own familiar world.

Such are some of the new strands which are making their appearance in the traditional pattern of Spanish society. Before we look more closely at them, we must turn to the historical and cultural influences of which this pattern itself is richly woven.

2   Cross and Crescent

BY THE TIME THE ROMAN LEGIONARIES made their appearance south of the Pyrenees in 218 BC, the Iberian Peninsula had
already witnessed a long succession of population movements, and
varied cultural achievements whose impressive vestiges survive to
excite our admiration today. The famous cave paintings of Altamira,
in the northern province of Santander, were probably completed
some fifteen thousand years before the birth of Christ. The men who
built the remarkable dolmens of Antequera and the *talayots* of the
Balearic Islands – huge slabs laid horizontally on stone uprights or
forming circular burial chambers – flourished sometime between the
sixth and second millennia BC. Soon after this period, the Celts had
begun to push southwards across the Pyrenees, establishing themselves most permanently in what is now Galicia and Portugal, but
also leaving evidence of their presence in many other parts of Spain
in the form of refined metal work and in the remarkable stone boars
and bulls to be found at Guisando, near Avila, and elsewhere. In
their migrations the Celts clashed and mingled with the Iberians,
another people of uncertain provenance, who had settled mainly in
the east of Spain. Forming enclaves amongst the primitive stock of the
peninsula were the trading-posts set up by the more advanced Mediterranean peoples – first, the Phoenicians, then the Greeks – attracted
by the metals, fruits, cattle and other resources of the peninsula.

The principal and most westerly settlement of the Phoenicians was
on the site of the present Cadiz, where a flourishing city arose,
famed for its great temple dedicated to Baal-Melkarte, the Hercules of
Tyre, whose twin columns continued to tower over the Straits until
pulled down by a rapacious Moorish admiral in the year 1145.

The Greeks established themselves mainly in the south-east of the peninsula. The name of what appears to have been their chief city, Emporion ('market-place'), indicates that, like their rivals the Phoenicians, they were interested less in conquest than in commerce. But the Greek colonists also succeeded, as the Phoenicians could never do, in communicating to their rude neighbours something of their own superb creative energies. In sculpture, especially, the civilized Iberians (first referred to under this name by the Greeks) came to excel. A splendid example of their art is the head known as the *Lady of Elche*, after the town where it was discovered, now in the Prado Museum.

In the sixth century BC, the Phoenicians, hard pressed in the local wars, turned for help to the Carthaginians who answered the call. As was to happen more than once in future centuries, the newcomers stayed on to conquer, trade and settle. The next three centuries were a period of increasing Carthaginian dominance. Though their main interest was commercial, in the third century BC, when Carthage was grappling in a life and death struggle with Rome, the military importance of the peninsula came to be increasingly recognized. Spain was strategically situated for the conduct of operations against the Romans in Italy and Gaul, and her people were a splendid reservoir of manpower. The Second Punic War against Rome was occasioned by Hannibal's capture, after a desperately heroic resistance, of Saguntum, a city half-way up the east coast of Spain, which considered itself an ally of Rome. Despite the brilliant victories won on Italian soil by Hannibal's armies, of which the Andalusian cavalry, the Celt-Iberian infantry, and the Balearic slingers formed the backbone, the Roman legions were able to counterattack and destroy Carthaginian power by the close of the third century. They completed what the Carthaginians had begun but had not managed to achieve – the unification of the peninsula beneath one centralized power.

THE ROMANS AND VISIGOTHS

During the five centuries of Roman domination, Spain was shifted out of the African into the European orbit and her disparate tribes and communities were welded into the beginnings of one nation. Of this process many impressive monuments still remain; the amphi-theatres at Italica and Mérida, the circuses at Sagunto and Calahorra, the aqueducts at Mérida and Segovia and the thermal baths, trium-phal arches, temples, bridges and city walls without number. The map of Spain is criss-crossed with Roman roads and studded with cities of Roman foundation such as Leon (Legio Septima), Sara-gossa (Caesar Augusta), Cordova (Corduba) and Osuna (Urso).

The cultural influence of Rome was no less profound. The con-quered gradually acquired the speech, dress, mode of life and values of their conquerors, and began to accept their rights and duties as citizens of a state. They could stand for electoral office in the cities, where municipal life developed a vigour which subsequent invasions could not extinguish until the Emperor Charles V broke their independent spirit in the early sixteenth century. The highest offices of army and state stood open too to men of Spanish birth, and the emperors Trajan, Hadrian, Marcus Aurelius and Theodosius were all sons of the peninsula. Roman law gave Spain a uniform admini-stration of justice which, despite later modifications and interrup-tions, remains basic to her legal system today. Latin supplanted the native dialects (except Basque) and gradually evolved into the other romance tongues spoken today throughout the peninsula. Latin literature was enriched too by contributions from writers of Spanish birth; the two Senecas and Lucan from Cordova, Quintilian from Calahorra, Martial from Calatayud. The noble stoicism of the elder Seneca, which seemed to express the quintessence of the Spanish attitude to life, had a particularly strong appeal in Spain. His works were studied and freely plagiarized by Catholic authors, and the legend grew up that he had been secretly baptized, perhaps by St Paul himself.

Did St Paul ever visit Spain? In his Epistle to the Romans he writes that this was his intention, but whether he ever did so we do not know. Most Spaniards believe that it was not St Paul but St James who brought the gospel to their land, and that he was buried at Santiago de Compostela. Thus Christianity had begun to take root in Spain by the second century and steadily gained ground in spite of – perhaps because of – the persecutions under Valerian and Diocletian. This early heroic age of the Catholic Church in Spain is known to us through the Latin hymns of Prudentius which sing the praises of centurions who would no longer serve in a pagan army, of bishops who refused to sacrifice to the Gods, of Eulalia, the thirteen-year-old martyr of Mérida, and of Vincent, one of the nineteen martyrs of Saragossa, who taunted his tormentors and laughed as they stretched him on the rack. Cordova, Tarragona, Gerona, Barcelona, Alcalá, Saragossa each had their quota of saints. Seville honours the memory of Justa and Rufina, two girls of lowly birth who won a martyr's crown by smashing a pagan image and centuries later were seen by pious eyes hovering over the Cathedral to protect it. The passionate cult of saints and of their relics, particularly of the local saint whose miracle-working prowess is more effective than that of the patron saints of all other localities, remains a feature of Spanish life.

The early Spanish Church showed some of the features which were to characterize it in later centuries. A church council of around AD 306 laid down the severest penalties for adultery, apostasy and idolatry, and forbade Christians to marry or to work with Jews or heretics. In two leaders of this period we recognize the prototypes of a long line of distinguished figures; Hosius, Bishop of Cordova, the first of the great prelate-statesmen, who played a leading part in the conversion of the Emperor Constantine; Priscillian, Bishop of Avila, the first distinguished churchman to be executed on charges of witchcraft and heresy.

In the early fifth century, the barbarians from the north began to sweep down over the Pyrenees. The mastery of Spain passed to the Visigoths, the most romanized of the Germanic peoples, who entered the peninsula as invaders and stayed on as allies of the last weak Roman emperors of the West, and then of the Byzantine emperors, whose influence spread over the southern part of the peninsula. After clearing the land of the other Germanic tribes, the Visigothic kings established their court at Toledo and imposed a half-civilized military aristocracy on the crumbling structure of Hispano-Roman society. Appropriating two-thirds of the land for themselves, by right of conquest, the Visigothic chiefs lived on their estates at the head of their military households. As they retained the elective system of monarchy, which made for efficiency in war but for intrigue and turbulence in times of peace, they had plenty of opportunity to pursue their traditional pastime of fighting.

By the middle of the seventh century, the Visigothic conquerors had merged with the more numerous Hispano-Romans. The fusion of culture and institutions, as well as of races, is typified by the famous code known as the *Liber Judiciorum*, promulgated around 654, in which German law and custom is combined with Roman principles of justice. Visigothic art shows the same composite quality, Byzantine influence, as well as Roman, being apparent in such splendid specimens of the goldsmith's art as the bejewelled crosses and crowns which have come down to us. Of Byzantine origin too – for he was the son of the Governor of Cartagena – was the greatest scholar and Latinist of his day, St Isidore. Tireless as a founder of schools and monasteries, he has left in his literary work, written in Latin, a vast compendium of the learning, both secular and sacred, of his time and a rich source for our knowledge of Visigothic Spain. Spain, declares St Isidore, having first been blessed by her union with the people of Romulus, now celebrates her betrothal to the glorious nation of the Goths.

As a prince of the church, St Isidore had good reason to speak with warmth of the Visigoths, who, although Arians, came to realize that the Catholic Church could provide them with an institutional framework and moral authority over the people. Largely through the efforts of St Leander, Isidore's elder brother, King Recared announced his conversion to Catholicism. From subjection to an alien race and creed, the Church began to assume the status of partnership with the temporal power. The king convened a series of councils at Toledo which served both as synods and councils of state, where laymen might sign canons of excommunication and prelates pass decrees of banishment. Bishops ceased to be elected and were nominated by the king, who was the final court of appeal in ecclesiastical suits. The administration of the land, in short, might be described as a royal theocracy; an experiment in that alliance between Church and State which was later to characterize Spain in her age of greatness.

Yet despite its period of prosperity and splendour, which historians date from 562–681, the Visigothic kingdom was basically unstable. Some of the nobles proved reluctant to give up their Arian faith and sought alliance with the Franks against the Crown. The espousal of Catholicism intensified rather than moderated the natural violence of the Visigoths, which was vented in particular against their numer, ous Jewish subjects, despite the pleas of churchmen that conversion should be attempted by persuasion rather than force. The fanatical intolerance of the Visigoths reached its peak at the end of the seventh century when, on the charge that the Jews were plotting with their co, religionists in Morocco to establish a Mosaic state in Spain, the Crown took measures to reduce the entire Jewish community to slavery and to have their children forcibly brought up as Christians.

Following the dethronement of King Witiza, civil war broke out between the partisans of his young sons and those who supported the usurper Roderic, or Rodrigo. The Witiza faction turned for help to Mūsā ibn Nusair, Governor of North Africa, whose Berber sub, jects had recently embraced Islam. Legend attributes a key role in the affair to Count Julian, the Christian governor of Ceuta who, before capitulating to the Moslems, had sent his young daughter to be brought up in safety at the Visigothic court. There, the story goes, the girl had been ravished by Rodrigo. When the latter asked Julian for some hunting falcons from Africa, the dishonoured father replied darkly that he would send him falcons of such a kind, and in such number, as would surprise him. These falcons were Mūsā's Berber warriors.

THE MOSLEM INVASIONS

In 711, an expeditionary army crossed the Straits under the command of Mūsā's lieutenant Tāriq ibn Ziyād and landed at the rock which was to bear his name (Jabal, al, Tāriq: Gibraltar). Rodrigo's forces were routed and the Moors, who had been summoned to Spain as auxiliaries, saw that the whole country lay open before them. Mūsā, jealous of Tāriq's success, hastened across the Straits to take command in person. Within seven years, the whole peninsula had been won for the Crescent. The tide of Moslem conquest indeed swirled past the Pyrenees, where only a few seemingly insignificant bands of Christians still held out, and penetrated deep into France until checked by Charles Martel at Poitiers (733). These years marked a great turning point in the destinies of Spain. The Moslem invasion wrenched the peninsula back from the European into the African orbit. Almost simultaneously, and at first imperceptibly, there began the long process of the Reconquest, with its profound consequences for the shaping of the national character, institutions, and policies of the Spanish people. The interaction, as well as the clash, between these two Spains was to prove, as we shall see, of fundamental importance in the formation of a reunited Spain.

How can we account for the extraordinary speed of the Moslem conquest? How was it that a state so faithful to the Cross could bow so readily to the Crescent? Largely because the Visigothic kings, for all their martial prowess and the wise counsels of the Church hierarchy, could never count on support from any substantial section of their subjects. Their armies were made up partly of slaves, and a slave had only to run away from his master and embrace Islam to be accounted free. The large and resourceful Jewish community, savagely persecuted by the Christian kings, saw that their lot could only be better under the Moslem invaders whom they actively assisted. The mass of the people, many of them still imperfectly Christianized, were offered the choice of conversion to Islam or continuance in their old faith subject to the payment of a poll-tax and other disabilities. Not even the warlike Gothic nobility could always be depended upon to resist. Many came to terms with the Moslem invaders, either apostatizing or retaining a qualified independence under Moslem suzerainty.

The Moslem conquerors, generally described as *Moros* or Moors, were themselves very far from constituting a homogeneous nation. Tāriq's force consisted mainly of Berbers, primitive and hardy tribesmen from the hill-country behind the North African littoral, fanatically attached to their recently espoused creed, unruly, and fiercely independent. Mūsā's men were Arabs, sceptical, imaginative, scornful of their rough co-religionists, and quick to take to the softer ways of city life, but they were also divided amongst themselves by old inter-tribal feuds. The first decades after the Moslem conquest were characterized by constant dissensions, some of them serious.

Until the middle of the eighth century, al-Andalus – as the Arabs called their Spanish possessions – remained subject to the Caliphate at Damascus. When the Umayyads, the ruling dynasty at Damascus, were ousted by the Abbasids, one of their princes, known as al-Dajil, the Fugitive, succeeded in escaping the massacre of his kins-men and in reaching Spain where he secured recognition as Abd-ar-Rahmān I, head of an Umayyad Emirate independent politically (though not in matters of faith) of the Abbasid Caliphate. His reign was disturbed by Abbasid attempts to unseat him, and by the incursion of a Christian army under Charlemagne, who was repulsed before the walls of Saragossa and forced to return to France.

The independent Emirate of Cordova lasted for more than a cen-tury and a half and culminated in its transformation into a full-blown Caliphate, claiming supreme religious as well as political authority throughout al-Andalus. The splendour and prosperity achieved by the Cordova Caliphate were largely due to the out-standing personality and long reign, first as Emir and then as Caliph, of Abd-ar-Rahmān III (912–961). After first breaking the power of a chieftain of Visigothic descent, Umar-ibn-Hafsūn, Abd-ar-Rahmān built up his army into the most formidable military machine in western Europe, and his fleet into a navy second to none in the Mediterranean. They secured for him the mastery of the African littoral and enabled him to deal a series of crushing blows against the Christian kingdoms of northern Spain. The latter indeed man-aged to gain at least one resounding victory over him in the ebb and flow of campaigning, but, by the time of his death, his tactics of alternating fierce raids with diplomatic blandishments had left them so weak and divided that his cultured and peace-loving son, al-Hakam, had little to fear from them.

Under the nominal reign of al-Hakam's successor, Hishām II, Moslem power reached a new peak of aggression and threatened once more to engulf the peninsula. The real master of al-Andalus was not the Caliph but an official who rose from chamberlain to all-powerful minister and commander-in-chief, Ibn-Abī-Āmir, known amongst the Moslems as al-Mansūr, the Victorious, and amongst the Christians as Almanzor. No despot has ever risen to power by a more ruthless process of ousting protectors, betraying friends, eliminating rivals, and destroying rebels (including one of his own sons). Yet none was more fanatically orthodox in his piety. At his command, al-Hakam's splendid library was purged of its rare manuscripts, whilst the tyrant himself transcribed his own copy of the Koran which he carried with him and studied on his campaigns. Almanzor's armies penetrated deep into Christian territory and sacked cities as far afield as Barcelona, Leon, and Santiago.

Yet hardly had the dread Almanzor been carried to the tomb in 1002 than cracks began to appear in the imposing edifice of the Cordova Caliphate. Whilst his sons and subordinates battled for the succession, old racial animosities, held in check under Almanzor's stern rule, burst into flame. Only seven years after Almanzor's death, a combined army of Berbers and Castilians was putting Cordova to sack. The Caliphate dissolved into a congeries of petty principalities known as *taifas,* with their own 'kings', miniature armies and courts. The ever deepening political chaos and military impotence of the *taifas* left them at the mercy of the increasingly aggressive Christian kingdoms.

However, the Moslem princes had one last card to play. They called in the warlike tribesmen called Almoravides, who crossed the Straits and routed the Christians, and then proceeded to oust the Moslem princelings and to gain control of all the south of al-Andalus. They would have pushed up the eastern coast too, perhaps as far as the Pyrenees, had it not been for the military genius of Rodrigo Díaz de Vivar, the Cid of Spanish poetry and legend, who held Valencia in alliance with such Moslem princes as realized they had more to fear from their African co-religionists than from the Christians.

Nevertheless, the wave of Almoravide conquest was soon spent. After sweeping away the princes whom they looked upon as impious and decadent, the desert chieftains themselves grew corrupted by the softer climate of Andalusian life. And whilst their power ebbed, a

39

fresh explosion was building up from the inexhaustible reserves of African fanaticism. A warrior sect known as the Almohads or 'unitarians', fired with holy zeal to restore the pristine purity of Islam, dethroned the Almoravide Emperor in the Maghreb in 1146 – exactly sixty years after the Almoravide invasion. There followed years of intense fighting between Cross and Crescent for the mastery of the peninsula. The decisive battle of Navas de Tolosa (1212) shattered Moslem dreams of the military conquest of Spain once and for all. Under the two great warrior kings, Jaime I of Aragon, and Ferdinand III of Castile, the Christian Reconquest proceeded apace.

Though Islam's once mighty possessions in Spain were eventually reduced to the Kingdom of Granada, the tide of reconquest faltered; and for nearly two and a half centuries this Moslem enclave remained, with some fluctuation of frontiers, in the otherwise wholly Christian-dominated Spain. Partly, Granada owed its immunity to the reinforcements which reached it from time to time from Africa, but above all it survived by skilfully playing off its position between Castile (to whom it was formally tributary), Aragon, and Morocco. It was not until the closing decade of the fifteenth century that Castile, emerging from the anarchy of its civil wars and united with Aragon through Isabel's marriage to Ferdinand, took up once more the interrupted task. On the second of January 1492, the Moorish King of Granada capitulated to the Catholic Monarchs and the last vestige of Moslem power disappeared from the peninsula.

THE CIVILIZATION OF MOSLEM SPAIN
With the fall of Granada there vanished – though some elements survived to influence the developing culture of Christian Spain – a remarkable civilization. Though created by invaders from Africa, Moslem Spain was no less 'Spanish' than the Catholic Spain which gradually emerged at its expense. Its demographic basis differed little from that of the Christian kingdoms. Reliable statistics are lacking, but it seems unlikely that the influx of Arabs exceeded 50,000 or that the more numerous Berbers ever totalled more than a few

hundred thousand amongst an estimated population of up to six million.[4] The Emirs and Caliphs of Cordova customarily took slave girls of Christian origin as their concubines, and many inherited the fair complexions and blue eyes of their Basque or Galician mothers. Their Arab and Berber subjects also interbred freely with the autochthonous Visigothic-Roman-Iberian population.

We have already noted the differences of race, temperament and culture which set Arabs against Berbers, and as the years went by, the *muladíes*, or Islamized Spaniards, against Almoravide and Almo- had new-comers from Africa. Mūsā had set the precedent by giving his Arab nobles the highest offices and the most fertile lands, whilst the Berbers were assigned to the harsher meseta and the defence of the mountainous frontier against the Christians. Though the Berbers were later to establish their own dynasties and produce some scholars of distinction, most remained employed in military or agricultural duties. The larger estates were generally worked by slave labour toiling in conditions little better than those of the cattle they tended. More fortunate was often the lot of the domestic or military slaves, some of whom rose to positions of great power at court.

The organizers of the slave trade, as of other remunerative com- mercial transactions with the East, were the Jewish merchants. We have noted how the large Jewish community in Spain, persecuted by the Visigothic kings, welcomed the Moslem invaders. Like the conquered Christians, the Jews who desired to retain their faith could do so undisturbed under their own religious and judicial authorities, subject to the payment of a poll-tax and other civic disabilities. They lived on in large and flourishing communities, even in cities of their own, such as Lucena, between Granada and Málaga. Until they felt the lash of Almoravide and Almohad fanaticism, they were more generally tolerated in al-Andalus than in the Christian kingdoms. Many made their fortunes in trade and the farming of taxes. Some achieved eminence as scholars and physicians, and a few as high officials of the *taifa* courts. This was specially the case for a time in the Kingdom of Granada, until the overweening arrogance of one Jewish vizier provoked popular resentment and this led to a general pogrom of the local Jews.

The Christians of al-Andalus were known as Mozarabs (moz-árabes). Their status varied according to the terms under which the Gothic nobles had first recognized Moslem suzerainty and the mood of the ruling Moslem prince. They were seldom subject to pressure to apostatize, for the poll- and land-taxes which they paid were a valuable source of state income. Living under their own *condes* and bishops, the Mozarabs were free to continue worshipping in their churches, though the principal one was generally taken over and turned into a mosque. By the middle of the ninth century, there were still six churches and two monasteries in the outskirts of Cordova and half a dozen more in the neighbouring sierra. Yet though they were not persecuted, the Mozarabs found themselves despised. As Islamic culture flowered, their own withered; their vernacular became adulterated or displaced by Arabic, and they came to adopt Moslem clothes and habits. The few whose faith remained fervent were prone to a hysteria which sought escape from frustration in voluntary martyrdom. Cordova, in the middle of the ninth century, witnessed harrowing scenes when monks, priests, young sol-diers, matrons and unmarried girls vied with each other in formally blaspheming the name of the prophet and thus incurring the koranic penalty of death. The Moslem authorities, fearing the risk of a general mozarabic revolt, tried to discourage the would-be martyrs by reasoning, ridicule and corrective lashes. But the mood of religious hysteria went on producing its victims until, in 859, the erudite Eulogius, Bishop-elect of Toledo, closed the roll of honour with the sacrifice of his life.

Apart from such outbursts, the Mozarabs gave little trouble in the first centuries of Moslem rule. They supplied the Caliph with some of his most loyal troops, and were to be found serving even under the banners of the dread Almanzor. It was only as the Reconquest advanced, and intolerance grew on each side, that the Mozarabs came to look to the Christians of the North for their salvation. Alfonso VI's Castilian cavalry would hardly have been able to operate so long and so freely in enemy territory without the support of the local Mozarab communities; but when his armies at length withdrew, thousands of them migrated to Christian territory to escape Moslem vengeance. These refugees, steeped in the ways of the Moors, were to become an important element in the Christian population, whilst the Mozarabs who remained in Moslem territory declined in numbers and cultural vigour.

The structure of Moslem society, until its fragmentation into the taifa kingdoms, was a pyramid with the Caliph, vested with full religious and secular authority, at its apex. His executive powers were exercised through a *hājib* or chief minister generally chosen from one of the four principal Arab families and other high officials (viziers) all appointed and dismissed at will. He also nominated – sometimes against their will – the *qadis*, with judicial powers of life and death. We know from a collection of anecdotes which has come down to us, *The Book of the Judges of Cordova*, that the qadi's office was often filled by men of notable probity and prudence. In cases where the accused happened to be himself an official of exceptionally high rank, an *ad hoc* judge known as the *sahib al mazalim* or 'master of oppressions' would be nominated to act as a sort of ombudsman. Law and order, the regulation of the markets, guilds and trade, and other aspects of civil life were supervised by special officials with a competence in advance of anything known to the Spaniards of the Christian kingdoms. The Spanish word for mayor, *alcalde* (derived from *qadi*), must not however lead us into supposing that the Moors had anything in the nature of elected municipal office. There were no town-halls in the Moslem cities, which lacked the autonomous life they had known under the Romans, and which they gradually re-acquired in Christian Spain.

The cities of al-Andalus, with their mosques and palaces, their inns, public baths and markets, were thriving and sometimes splendid places. Seville, Málaga, Almería, and other ports developed a lively commerce with Africa, North Europe and the Near East, some merchants venturing on even to the Far East. The Moors gave a new impulse to Spain's traditional crafts and industries, such as the metal-work of Toledo and the mines of Andalusia. Almería, Málaga, Granada and Murcia became famous for their silks, whilst Játiva was producing and exporting paper long before its use became general in Europe. In agriculture the Moors were especially skilled;

to them Spain owes the introduction of such crops as cotton, rice and sugar-cane, and the careful cultivation of figs, dates, peaches, apricots, pomegranates, lemons and oranges.

The centre of all this prosperity, until the collapse of the Caliphate at the beginning of the eleventh century, was the great city of Cordova, famous for its carpets, its leather work, its priceless woven fabrics, and its exquisitely wrought ivories. Al-Shaqundī, author of a eulogistic poem *On the Excellency of al-Andalus*, describes Cordova as 'the seat of empire, the centre of science, the beacon of religion and the abode of nobility and leadership', and says that when he visited it he rode through ten miles of 'uninterrupted buildings along a road lit by lamps from end to end'.[5] Its supreme glory was the great mosque built on the site of a Christian church by Abd-ar-Rahmān I and enlarged by his successors down to the time of Almanzor. This mosque is now a Catholic Cathedral. The interpolation of altar and choir-stalls amidst the stately avenues of horseshoe and foiled arches, with their alternation of red and yellow dowels, strikes a note of incongruity which is the price paid for the preservation, down to our own day, of this otherwise intact masterpiece of early Spanish Moslem art.

Time has dealt less kindly with the other great monument of Moslem Cordova. This is the palace-city of Madīnat-az-Zahrā which Abd-ar-Rahmān III built a few miles outside Cordova to serve as the administrative and ceremonial headquarters of the Caliphate. Here architects, craftsmen, and artists from Baghdad and Constantinople joined with those of Cordova to produce a series of buildings forming a harmonious synthesis of Umayyad tradition and Byzantine features. Destroyed by the Berbers soon after its com-pletion and ransacked by subsequent generations, the 'Flower-City' of the Caliphs is now once more, thanks to skilful excavation and restoration, beginning to reveal something of its ancient splendours.

If Madīnat-az-Zahrā and the great mosque of Cordova mark the inspired starting point for the development of a Spanish and Islamic art, the Alhambra at Granada is its incomparable swan song. Built as a fortress, royal residence and administrative centre for the last of the Moorish kingdoms, it rises over the city in ascending terraces on a spur of the Sierra Nevada. The Alhambra blends with the enchanted Andalusian landscape as if to symbolize the Moors' attachment to the soil of Spain, which they refused to surrender to the Christians encamped around them. The palace merges into its gardens, its chambers melting into patios which in turn become terraces or garden paths, its walls dissolving into loggias and arcades, while rills and formal pools and fountain jets link together foliage, sky and soaring stone into a miraculous ethereal harmony. There is something fragile and nostalgic about the Alhambra which has appealed strongly to romantic writers like Chateaubriand and Washington Irving and still affects the casual tourist of today. We feel, as we gaze upon the miracles of intricate and ingenious decoration which cover those walls, that we are looking upon the final stages of a culture dominated not only by the enemy at its gates but by the memory of its own greatness. The urge to create and experiment is spent; only the concern to preserve, refine and elaborate remains. Architecture itself has become a framework for decorative virtuosity.

There is something of this same quality in the poetry so much in vogue throughout Moslem Spain, specially in the taifa courts. Islamic poetry is a highly formalized art, ruled by strict convention as to theme and structure, which leaves the poet free to shine only in the brilliance, subtlety and intricacy of his verbal arabesques. A eulogistic ode by a poet of repute was valued by a prince as a means of enhancing his prestige. A well-turned couplet could make its author's fortune or bring ruin to an enemy. The pogrom of Jews in Granada mentioned earlier is said to have been triggered off by a *faqih's* venomous verses. Mu'tamid, the poet-king of Seville, was one day amusing himself composing verses with a companion by the banks of the Guadalquivir when a slave girl, who happened to be washing her clothes in the river, interposed a neat line. The girl was as beautiful as she was witty, so Mu'tamid married her and remained devoted to her throughout his life, even finding time to pen poems to her in the thick of his campaigns. The people had their own songs and poems, entirely different from the mannered compositions of the court. Two of these popular verse-forms, however, the *muwashshah* and the *zéjel*, were taken up by the aristocratic poets and eventually broke into the charmed circle of accepted literary genres. The interesting thing about them is that they not only combined classical with colloquial Arabic, but even included lines in the Romance vernacular. These fragments are the embryos of Spanish literature, and afford striking evidence of the interplay of Hispanic and Moorish elements in the popular culture of medieval Spain.

The greatest poet and writer of al-Andalus was probably Ibn Hazm of Cordova, who served for a time as vizier following the break-up of the Caliphate, but withdrew to devote the rest of his life to study and writing. He clashed with the rigid Malikite jurists who condemned his books to the flames – an action which elicited from their author a fine poem of pride and defiance, and which reminds us that Moslem, no less than Catholic, Spain had its inquisition. Ibn Hazm's most remarkable works are the love poems contained in *The Dove's Ring*, which has been translated into the major European languages, his collection of maxims, character sketches and autobiographical confessions, and his learned but polemical treatise on the Islamic schools, Judaism and Christianity. Some scholars attribute a characteristically 'Spanish' quality to the work of this proud, passionate, irascible, but noble-hearted seeker after truth, and find in it echoes of the lofty stoicism of his fellow-Cordovan Seneca and anticipations of the moralizing and soul-searching of such profoundly Catholic writers as Quevedo and Unamuno.

In the philosophical writings of Ibn Bajja (Avempace), Ibn Tufayl, and the famous Ibn Rushd (Averroes) and in many other fields of learning – in mathematics and astronomy, in medicine, in works of geography, history, philosophy, and Islamic exegesis and jurisprudence – the scholars of al-Andalus made notable contributions. That these often derived from greater and more original works created in the Islamic heartlands scarcely diminishes the value of their achievement. The Spanish Moslems were the great middlemen of culture, transmitters of the learning of the ancient world all but forgotten in the West but, for Islamic scholars, a source of close study and creative stimulus. European scholarship owes a special debt to Toledo where, with the enlightened encouragement of King Alfonso the Learned, Moslem, Jewish and Christian scholars collaborated

for over a century in the production of Latin and vernacular translations of a rich variety of scientific and philosophical texts. Through
Spain too, Europe was probably introduced to such widely different
inventions as paper, gunpowder and Arabic numerals. The Mozarabs
and later the *mudéjares* promoted familiarity with Moorish ways and
skills. The Christian princes themselves, even when warring against
the Moors, affected much of their more sophisticated style of living.

What Moslem elements have entered into the psychology of the
Spanish family or found a permanent place in their national heritage?
When a Spaniard of today says that he will do something *si Dios
quiere* – if God wills – or would that this, that, or the other may be so –
ojalá, may Allah grant it! – or assures you that his house is yours, he
is expressing the eastern turn of phrase which comes naturally to his
lips. His language is full of words of clearly Arabic origin, particularly those relating to trade, handicrafts and buildings, to military
matters and objects of household use, to agriculture, crops and fruits.
And beneath these vestiges of Moslem influence we may sometimes
glimpse the deeper imprint left on the national psychology by the
centuries of conflict and coexistence which Spaniards call the
Reconquista.

THE CHRISTIAN RECONQUEST
The first puzzle is why the Reconquest should have happened at
all. Why, of all the provinces of the western Roman Empire overrun
by the Moslems, should it have been only in Spain that a handful of
unorganized survivors fought back against a power of initially
overwhelming superiority, until the whole peninsula was at last
reincorporated in western Christendom? Was it out of a sense of
loyalty to the Visigothic–Iberian tradition, and a desire to restore it?
But the nuclei of resistance appeared in the borderlands where the
Visigothic writ had scarcely run, and the new Christian states which
began to emerge differed considerably in spirit from the old Visigothic Kingdom. Was it due to the influence of their Frankish
neighbours to the North? But when Charlemagne was the supreme
power in western Christendom and involved in north-eastern
Spain, the small Christian kingdoms refused an alliance with him.

It is easier to say how, rather than why, the Reconquest occurred. The first independent foothold which the Christians secured for themselves was the tiny Kingdom of Asturias, formed by a Visigothic chieftain called Pelayo after inflicting on the Moslems their first defeat. By the end of the eighth century the Christians had regained enough ground to establish their capital at Oviedo. Other enclaves of Christian territory had in the meantime come into existence in the mountains of Navarre and Aragon. Charlemagne, as we have noted, failed to include northern Spain within the frontiers of his empire, but a Frankish province known as the Spanish March was organized by his son, Louis the Pious, in what is now Catalonia.

By the early tenth century, the Asturian Kingdom had been exten-ded to include Galicia, Burgos and Leon, the latter city becoming the new capital, and Ordoño II (914–24) taking the title of King of Leon. The Christians had now reached the river Duero, which was for long to mark the frontier with Islam. But the mounting power of the Cordovan Caliphate checked the Christian advance. Alman-zor's armies invaded and sacked Leon, which was repopulated only after his death. Castiella or Castile, the castle-studded zone which bore the brunt of the ceaseless warfare, was subdivided into 'counties' under counts or condes appointed by the king to organize its defence. These counts grew steadily more independent of the royal power and chose two of their number as 'judges' to vindicate their rights against Leon. It has been suggested that Castile owed its more mili-tant spirit to the fact that its population was composed mainly of hardy highlanders whereas that of Leon had been formed chiefly from Mozarabs resettled from the Moorish lands.[6] Castile's mili-tary efficiency was also increased by granting noble rank, with the privileges and tax exemptions which went with it, to the class of small landowners known as *infanzones*. This strengthened the cavalry arm and broadened the vigorous democratic basis of Castilian society. Under Fernán González, the most outstanding of the counts and the hero of a famous medieval epic, Castile attained virtual inde-pendence, though it only acquired the formal status of a kingdom, after temporary absorption into the expanded kingdom of Sancho the Great, under the latter's son Fernando I in 1035.

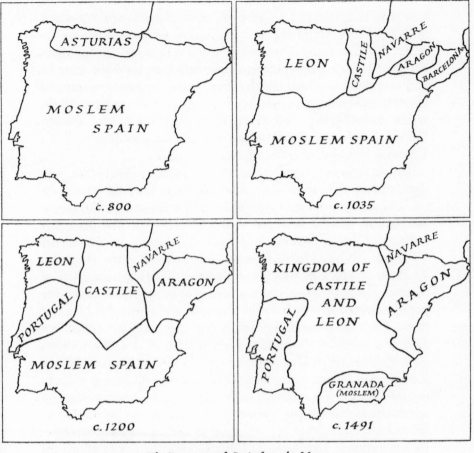

The Reconquest of Spain from the Moors

A process of kaleidoscopic fragmentation and regrouping now set in when the Christian kingdoms – Leon (with Asturias and at times Galicia), Navarre, Castile and Aragon – together with the counties of the Spanish March (of which the County of Barcelona had emerged as the strongest) strove to increase their territories at the expense of their Christian and Moorish neighbours. These kingdoms subdivided their possessions at death, so that the larger units were constantly dissolving into smaller ones and brothers fought to secure each other's inheritance. After the break-up of the Caliphate, the

Christian kings devised a system of 'zones of reconquest' by which individual taifa kingdoms were earmarked for acquisition by the competing Christians. The technique was to force an 'alliance' upon a weaker Moslem prince, extorting tribute money from him until he had alienated his subjects by the heavy taxes imposed on them and found himself obliged to cede key fortresses, or even the throne itself, to his insatiable liege. However, it was not easy to find enough Christian settlers to repopulate the war-devastated areas or to give a Christian character to ceded Moslem townships.

The conditions prevailing in eleventh-century Spain are well illustrated by the career of the Cid. Rodrigo Díaz de Vivar (the title *Cid* derives from the term *sidi*, lord, by which he was known to his Moslem vassals) belonged to the *infanzón* class and his extra-ordinary military prowess won him the enmity of the higher Castilian nobility. His exploits are immortalized in the great epic *El Poema de Mío Cid*, which is the earliest surviving masterpiece of Spanish literature. He is also the hero of innumerable *romances*, the popular ballads in which Spain is so rich, and of many subsequent plays. This later material is generally quite legendary in content, but there is a considerable basis of historic truth in the *Poema* which gives us a stirring and fascinating picture of medieval Spain. We see Church and Nation being forged into one, and the idea of a Spain regained for the Cross already taking shape as the national ideal. It shows the important part played by the monasteries in helping to consolidate and restore the economy of the reconquered territory; the monastery of San Pedro de Cardeña, near Burgos, to which the Cid entrusts his wife and daughters and where he is himself at last laid to rest, figures prominently in the epic. We hear the Christian knights uttering their battle cry of 'Santiago,' as they clash with Moors invoking the help of Mahomet. This cult of St James forms an important and fascinating strand running through much of Spanish history.[7] The belief which transforms the apostle of Galilee into Santiago Matamoros, St James the Moorslayer, patron saint of Spain, seems to have evolved as a counterpart to the religious militancy of Islam. A famous document known as the Diploma of Ramiro I, purporting to date from the ninth century but probably forged by monks in the twelfth in order to justify the collection of a tax as thank-offering, described how the saint, riding a white horse and flourishing a flashing sword, appeared to rally the faltering Christians at the battle of Clavijo and turned their defeat into victory. St James was subsequently reported to appear in like fashion at other crucial moments in Spanish history: at the surrender of Coimbra in 1064, at the decisive battle of Navas de Tolosa, even in the Italian campaigns of the Great Captain Gonzalo de Córdoba and in the conquest of Mexico by Cortés. What is certain is that the discovery of the reputed tomb of St James had turned Santiago de Compostela into one of Christendom's most venerated shrines and opened up the famous route, trod by *juglares* (minstrels), pilgrims and adventurers of every description, which was to prove the most important artery for the transmission of reciprocal influences between Spain and Northern Europe throughout the Middle Ages.

The belief that Christianity could triumph by force of arms was characteristic of medieval Europe in general. It led to the Crusades, the counterpart of the Moslem concept of the *jihad*, or holy war. It produced the warrior monks of the Military Orders (of which Spain developed its own variants in the Orders of Santiago, Alcántara, Calatrava and others) as Islam produced the fanatical ascetics who garrisoned the *ribat*. But nowhere did this militant spirit find fuller expression than in Spain where, as a Spanish king once declared, 'we are always on crusade'. Its embodiment is the great figure of Ferdinand III of Castile – San Fernando Rey – king and canonized saint, whose life was devoted to the twin ideals of military reconquest and personal sanctity. He ended the old rivalry between Castile and Leon, which were henceforth to remain united beneath one crown, and after conquering Seville, avoided what looked like an inevitable clash with the other advancing power of the Reconquest, Aragon.

The face of Christian Spain was now changing. Not only did the thirteenth century see its expansion at the expense of the Moslems, but the crystallization of its small component units into three blocks; Castile (including Leon), Aragon-Catalonia (including the county of Barcelona) and Portugal. The latter had become a separate kingdom around 1140, and the determination which its subjects showed in retaining their own language, institutions, and political independence, despite repeated attempts by Castile to absorb it, assured for it a destiny quite distinct from that of the rest of the peninsula. Not so with Aragon-Catalonia. That kingdom also looked beyond the peninsula to its future, building up a flourishing Mediterranean trade based on an advanced code of maritime law (*Consolat de la mar*), establishing a sort of protectorate over Tunisia, conquering Sicily (1284), Sardinia (1324), Naples (1443) and even for a time extending its power to Asia Minor and the Duchy of Athens (1326–87). But it never severed its connection with Castile. With the latter, it is true, the relationship was generally one of tension and frustration from the time that the Aragonese nobles refused to follow King Jaime in a joint campaign which might have completed the Reconquest on the plea that they were not obliged to serve the King of Castile. Nor did matters improve when, on the extinction of the royal line, the throne of Aragon passed (1412) to Ferdinand of Antequera, a prince whose virtues could not, in their eyes, override the fact that he was a Castilian. Differences of national tradition and temperament had already left their stamp upon the peoples of the two kingdoms. 'Ferdinand and his Castilians are not free, as we are', summed up the feeling of Aragon. And to demonstrate how free and independent they were, the new king was compelled, like any of his subjects, to pay the local taxes prescribed by the *fueros* of Barcelona.

The chartered rights and privileges known as *fueros* were an important feature of medieval Spain. They had developed naturally in the course of the Reconquest, as the Crown needed to repopulate the lands and cities recovered. They varied in their terms according to locality and historical context, the more liberal fueros being specifically open to Jews and Moslems as well as Christians. Thanks to these charters, the towns became a vigorous new force in the realm, electing their own officers and increasingly managing their affairs, even to the extent of raising their own militia and banding themselves together in confederations. A communal system thus grew up in Spain side by side with a modified feudal system. In its struggle to impose the royal authority on a turbulent nobility, the Crown frequently allied itself with the municipalities who were themselves constantly at odds with their secular and ecclesiastical overlords over the defence or extension of their fueros. When, in the early sixteenth century, the Crown succeeded in breaking the power of the nobles, it moved to crush in turn that of the municipalities. The royal absolutism of imperial Spain was thus reared on the ruins of an older, more democratic tradition which it has been the dream of Spanish liberal reformers to revive.

Another expression of the medieval democratic spirit – or more exactly, of the corporate endeavour of king, nobles, churchmen and common people to conduct their affairs in common – was the development of parliaments or *cortes*, summoned to decide on succession to the throne and to raise money. Since the Church and nobility had the privilege of paying no taxes, the municipalities were virtually the only source of taxable wealth and their representatives were required to take their place beside the nobles and prelates. Exactly when the practice of holding a cortes began it is impossible to say; they are on record in Castile in 1250, in Leon in 1188 and in Aragon perhaps as early as 1163; at all events, well before the first fully fledged parliaments in England.

The thirteenth century was thus a time of great achievement and splendid promise in Spain. Except for the small kingdom of Granada, the whole peninsula had been reconquered for the Cross. The Church had been re-invigorated, thanks largely to the reforms introduced by monks from the great French monastery of Cluny (though at the cost of substituting the Roman liturgy for the Visigothic or 'Mozarabic' rite traditionally in use in Spain). The towns were promoting the growth of trade and a more settled way of life, whilst the people's attachment to their fueros and the influence of their cortes augured well for the development of individual liberties and representative institutions. But the fourteenth, and much of the fifteenth, centuries marked an age of decline and confusion, not only in Spain but throughout much of Christendom – an age of plague and famine, feudal strife and peasant revolts. To note the decline we have only to compare the spirit of a Ramon Lull (1233-1315), the Mallorcan sage, mystic and missionary, with that of the worldly-wise Archpriest of Hita (d. circa 1350), author of the *Libro de Buen Amor*, whose amorous adventures include an account of how he was sent to exhort the clergy of Talavera to put away their concubines. In Castile, Alfonso the Learned was deposed by his turbulent nobles, and Alfonso XI, last of the strong medieval rulers, carried off by the plague. Under Pedro the Cruel (1350-69) the land sank into misery and anarchy which deepened into civil war after the death of the weak Enrique IV (1474). The rival claimants to the throne were his putative daughter Juana, and Enrique's sister Isabel. In Aragon, strife between king and nobles had been followed by a long and terrible rising of the exploited peasantry. Peace was at last restored by the astute young King Ferdinand II, who some years before had married Isabel of Castile. When, in 1476, that princess emerged victorious from the struggle for the succession, the way was open for the partnership of Castile and Aragon beneath the rule of the royal consorts. The prelude of long and painful gestation was over, and the curtain was about to rise on a unified Spain destined for the mastery of the world stage.

3   The Golden Age

THE EMERGENCE OF SPAIN as a world power was dramatic enough to cause Machiavelli to note that Ferdinand, whom he admired as the prototype of his 'new prince', had transformed himself 'from a small and weak king into the greatest monarch in Christendom'. Energies which had for centuries been absorbed in warfare against the Moors or in internecine strife suddenly found new and creative outlets. The nation – and perhaps we can now begin to speak of the Spaniards as consciously one nation – seemed suddenly to have become aware of the magnificent destiny awaiting it. The *annus mirabilis* of 1492, which marked the end of the *Reconquista*, also witnessed the start of the epic of the *Conquista* and of Spain's empire in the New World. The same year saw too the expulsion of the Jews, the earnest of the Crown's determination to make Catholic orthodoxy the chief unifying force of its expanding realms. Spain, hitherto little more than a geographical expression, was soon to be epitomized in the phrase 'One King, one Empire, one Sword'.

THE STRUCTURE OF GOVERNMENT

But, first, the Crown had to consolidate its own power. The marriage of Isabel and Ferdinand, whom history knows as the *Reyes Católicos* or Catholic Monarchs, meant that Castile and Aragon were to be ruled by the same sovereigns even though they had not yet become one kingdom. Each retained its own laws and institutions. In Castile, Ferdinand at first made a bid for the throne on his own account, but Isabel, for all her wifely affection, could be firm where her own rights were concerned and vindicated her primacy. Thereafter, as far as

55

possible, the consorts exercised authority jointly, their personal qualities admirably complementing each other; Ferdinand, tenacious,
energetic, calculating and close-fisted, Isabel, prudent and scrupu-
lous, deeply pious and capable of inspiring affectionate devotion as
well as obedience. Both were united in their resolve to strengthen
the monarchy and both had a flair for choosing men who would
serve them well.

The Catholic Monarchs knew the art of inspiring their subjects
with an enthusiastic sense of cooperation in the national purpose.
Years of anarchy had accustomed the Castilian nobility to follow
their own devices rather than the sovereign's will, so Isabel and
Ferdinand set about bringing them firmly to heel. Their grants and
annuities were scrutinized and largely revoked; the power and wealth
of the great Military Orders were secured for the Crown by having
their grand-masterships conferred upon Ferdinand; the great nobles
saw key posts in government increasingly filled by men of more humble
birth and proven professional ability – the *letrados*, priests or lawyers,
trained in Spain's now flourishing universities. In this struggle
with the nobles the Crown's staunchest allies were the municipalities
which had long been fighting to assert their rights against seigniorial
pretensions. The levies which the medieval cities had raised to protect their interests and maintain law and order were expanded by the
Crown into an efficient national force, the *Santa Hermandad* or Holy
Brotherhood, for the repression of banditry or the lawlessness of
local magnates.

The foundations were also laid for the establishment of a new and
formidable military machine. The Granada campaign, though lit by
romantic episodes between Moorish and Christian knights, was
really won by the systematic reduction of enemy strong-points by the
Spanish siege artillery; the pips of the pomegranate, as Ferdinand
put it, had to be eaten one by one. In Italy, the infantry was reorgan-
ized by the military genius of Gonzalo de Córdoba. The phalanxes
of Spanish pikemen, supported by arquebusiers and mobile swords-
men and javelin-throwers, proved irresistible. In tactics, equipment,
élan, and stamina, the *tercios* were to dominate the battlefields of
Europe for a century and a half.

The establishment of Spanish power in the New World followed a different pattern. The Conquista was a joint enterprise between the Crown and private individuals. In an agreement known as a *Capitulación*, the Crown authorized the expedition concerned and specified the conquistador's rights of exploration, conquest and colonization and the financial rewards and privileges he might expect from its success. The conquistador, on his side, undertook to raise the armed force and cover the expenses of the expedition (sometimes in collaboration with the Crown). This was essentially the practice followed in the medieval war against the Moors, and shows the intimate connection between Reconquista and Conquista. The setting aside for the Crown of the important 'Royal Fifth' of all booty taken, and later of all gold and silver produced in the mines, itself stems from accepted Moslem practice. The success of Spain's military enterprises in the New World depended largely on the bold leadership and resourcefulness of individual adventurers acting under royal licence. The key arm was not the infantry, as in Europe, but the cavalry, a handful of which might suffice to overawe or run down a host of lightly armed natives. 'After God', wrote Bernal Diaz del Castillo, the soldier-chronicler of the conquest of Mexico, 'our trust was in our horses'.

The establishment and administration of the royal power in newly conquered territories separated from the metropolis by immense distances followed lines laid down by the Catholic Monarchs and practised in their European dominions. Though Isabel and Ferdinand strove to consolidate the royal power, they did not attempt to do so by fusing Castile and Aragon into one, or even by reducing their differing institutions to conformity. In Aragon, the King's freedom of action remained limited by the rights of the respective Cortes of Catalonia, Valencia and Aragon proper. A special official, the Justicia Mayor, acted as a sort of ombudsman between the king and his subjects and administered an oath of grudging loyalty in the famous formula: 'We, who are just as good as you, swear to you, who are no better than ourselves, to accept you as our king and sovereign lord, provided you observe all our liberties and laws; but if not, not.' It was expected of the king that he should be normally resident in his kingdom. Since his preoccupations in Castile and Italy made this manifestly impossible, the office of viceroy was devised. This proved a valuable institution which was extended to the other royal domains, so that in time the number of viceroyalties rose to nine; Aragon, Valencia, Catalonia, and Navarre in the peninsula; Sardinia, Sicily and Naples, in the Mediterranean; New Spain and Peru in the New World. Linking viceroy and monarch, advising the latter and transacting general business pertaining to the kingdom concerned, was the Council. Evolving from medieval prototypes, these Councils were to prove a flexible if cumbersome instrument of royal control as new territories came under the Crown or new areas of national life called for administrative ordering. They were to form in time the chief mechanism of Spain's imperial bureau cracy. Bodies like the Council of the Indies and the Council of Finance performed functions similar to those of powerful ministries. But for one there was no such equivalent anywhere outside Spain; The Council of the Inquisition.

THE INQUISITION

During the centuries of combat and confrontation with Islam, the Church had become identified with the Spanish nation. It had contributed powerfully, both in inspiration and material resources, to the Reconquista. Nor had the great prelates hesitated to take sides, like any other nobles, in the civil wars; Archbishop Mendoza of Seville had fought for Isabel, Archbishop Carrillo of Toledo for her rival. The Catholic Monarchs realized the need for both revitaliz ing the Church spiritually and for bringing it institutionally more fully under their control. The first was an aim particularly dear to the pious Queen; the second led, particularly in the reigns of Charles V and Philip II, to a state of undeclared, and sometimes open, warfare with the Papacy over such matters as the right to make appointments to ecclesiastical office. After the fall of Granada this right of *patronato* in the newly won territories was conceded to the Crown and later extended to Spain's vast dominions throughout the New World.

The Catholic Monarchs had offered generous terms to the defenders of Granada. The Moslems were to retain their property, their own magistrates, their laws and customs and their religion. Hernán de Talavera, the Queen's confessor and a man of saintly character, was appointed Archbishop of Granada and won the hearts of the people by the respect he showed for their rights and by the gentle fervour of his example and eloquence. But the Santiago spirit was not to be gainsaid; pressure mounted for the uncompromising and immediate victory of the Cross over the Crescent. The Queen came increasingly under the influence of her new confessor Francisco Ximénez de Cisneros, whose religious zeal pressed for mass conversion and a holocaust of the Moslems' sacred books. The outcome was a serious riot in Granada, quelled through Talavera's mediation, and a rising of the Moorish villagers of the Sierra Nevada, which Ferdinand suppressed with fire and sword. The defeated rebels were given the option of expulsion or conversion. The Church was left with the problem of assimilating a mass of nominally Christian 'Moriscos', resentful and tenaciously attached in secret to their ancient faith. Spain had taken one step further towards religious and political unification, but the price paid was the abandonment of the medieval tradition of tolerance and the alienation of a large and industrious section of the population, culminating in the expulsion of the Moriscos in 1609. It also marked the eclipse of that spirit of charity, tolerance and mutual respect which had drawn Jewish, Moslem and Christian scholars together in their joint work of translation at Toledo, and had brought men of the three faiths together to worship in the same city beneath the common roof of Santa María la Blanca.

The fate of the Jews was no less tragic. They had known persecution under the Visigoths; then tolerance under the Moslems and later, increasingly, in the Christian kingdoms they had come to constitute the bulk of the middle class as well as furnishing many valued royal advisers and officials, especially in the administration of finances. The latter activity, coupled with the growing wealth and influence of the predominantly Jewish merchant class, aroused widespread popular resentment which was liable to burst out from time to time in fierce pogroms. A nation which was finding its unity and sense of national destiny in a militant faith was less and less prepared to tolerate an alien religious minority within its midst. Many Jews, it is true, had embraced Christianity. Some of these *conversos* or 'new Christians' had risen to high office in the church and were often – like Talavera himself and not a few of the great Catholic mystics – men of sincere spirituality. But for others, conversion had been a matter of expediency, and they were liable to lapse either deliberately or for lack of proper instruction in the Christian faith, or merely by the retention of certain inborn habits which appeared to the old Christians as sinister 'Judaizing tendencies'. The expulsion of all practising Jews in 1492 was designed to shield the conversos from a standing temptation to lapse and – as with the measures later taken against the Moslems – as a means of cementing national unity. But expulsion was not enough. The orthodoxy of the conversos themselves had to be rigorously watched and any backsliding pun/ ished. To this end the Catholic Monarchs petitioned the Pope in 1478 for a bull establishing the Inquisition in Spain.

Medieval Christendom had had its Inquisitors, but only for limited periods and areas, where some particular heresy – such as that of the Albigensians in the south of France – needed to be suppressed. That crisis had seen the emergence of a Spanish monk, St Domingo Guzmán, as the foremost champion of orthodoxy and it was the Order of Preachers which he founded that now served as the general staff of the new Inquisition. The latter differed from its predecessors in that it was designed as a permanent and nation/wide institution answerable to the Crown rather than the Pope. The Catholic Mon/ archs were not motivated by anti/Semitic prejudice. They continued to employ conversos amongst their closest advisers, and Ferdinand himself had Jewish blood in his veins. Because they had made religious conformity the touchstone of national unity, the Inquisition soon became almost as much a political as a religious institution. Aimed originally against backsliding into Islam and Judaism, it was later to prove, where heretics became equated with rebels, an instru/ ment of terrible efficiency for the suppression of any glimmering of Protestantism. So great and arbitrary did its power become, that a Primate of all Spain, Archbishop Carranza of Toledo, could be accused of heresy, arrested and brought to a trial which dragged on for seventeen years.

The establishment of this new arm of authoritarianism did not pass unchallenged. The tradition of tolerance was not yet dead and attachment to local and individual rights was strong. In Aragon, opposition was particularly fierce, and the newly appointed Inquisitor was assassinated. But the common people, it seems, came generally to approve as well as to fear the Holy Office. The victims of the Inquisition were for the most part better educated and better off (confiscation of goods rather than the salvation of souls could be a motive for inquisitorial attention) and the solemn spectacle of an *auto-da-fé* could not only exalt the religious emotions of the orthodox populace but also allowed it to sublimate the baser emotions of envy and class hatred which had previously erupted in spontaneous pogroms. Even people who had most to fear from the prying, the secrecy and interminable delays of its proceedings, its prisons, public humiliations and implacable punishments did not question the necessity of the Holy Office. The celebrated preacher and writer Luis de Granada, one of the many notable mystics who suffered in person or in their writings at the hands of the Holy Office, could still laud it with baroque fervour as 'the bastion of the Church, the pillar of truth, guardian of the faith, treasure of the Christian religion, an arm against heretics and a beacon against the deceits of the enemy'.[8]

Protestant writers have traditionally depicted the Inquisition as the centrepiece in the Black Legend of Spain's iniquities. Today, historians tend to judge it less harshly and to assure us that 'by the standards of the times, it was neither cruel nor unjust in its procedure and its penalties; in many ways it was more just and humane than almost any other tribunal in Europe'.[9] Yet can we deny that the Inquisition, through its network of informers and secret dossiers, its methods of interrogation ranging from physical torture to subtle brain-washing, and its carefully staged scenes of public confession, is the prototype of modern techniques of enforced ideological conformity? Though he would indignantly disclaim the paternity, the Inquisitor is the spiritual father of the Commissar. Apologists for the Inquisition – and there are still many today in Spain – maintain that the Index, the Censorship, and the inquisitorial apparatus for the suppression of any independent thought could have no harmful effects, since the heyday of the Holy Office was also Spain's golden age of artistic and intellectual creativity. But the truth is that the Inquisition shut off Spain from the outer world. In time no breath of fresh air was allowed in from a more sceptical but also a more vigorous Europe. Spain became asphyxiated and settled into a long decline. At first, however, there was no awareness of this danger. When the Catholic Monarchs reigned Spain was imbued with its awakening national energies, the stimulus of Renaissance thought and the new currents of European spirituality. Thus it was not from the stifling atmosphere of the Inquisition but from the freer climate of this earlier Spain that the country drew strength for its greatest achievements.

It has sometimes been debated whether the Renaissance had any influence at all in Spain. Certain forms of culture appear indeed to have gone on enduring from the Middle Ages with apparently little trace of the classical spirit; polychrome sculpture, mudéjar and later plateresque architecture (Gothic, with an exuberance of Moorish and Renaissance decorative motifs), Calderón's *autos sacramentales* (Baroque culmination of the medieval mystery plays) and, to some extent, the Spanish theatre which drew themes from the *romancero*. In the great figures of the age, medieval and humanistic traits were strangely blended. Cisneros, who had ordered the book-burnings and mass conversions of Granada and urged that a crusade be carried on into Africa, was also the enlightened founder of the University of Alcalá, and encouraged the University to complete its work on the Polyglot Bible. The Catholic Monarchs themselves were patrons of the new learning, which reached Spain through Ferdinand's Italian possessions. Isabel set the fashion for classical studies. Pietro Martire, the Italian humanist invited to the court to further the new interest in education, wrote, 'My house is all day full of young nobles who now realize that letters are not a hindrance but a help in the career of arms.' Above all, Spain responded to the stimulus of Erasmus. 'At the Emperor's court, in the towns, the churches, the monasteries, even in the inns and on the roads, everyone now has the Enquiridion of Erasmus', wrote the Spanish translator of the famous book.[10] Nevertheless, only up to a point could the questioning spirit of the sage of Rotterdam be tolerated. Friars smarting under his satire and conservatives who saw his influence behind the *alumbrados* quickly suppressed his teaching. Spain, unlike other countries of Europe, was not prepared to throw open her frontiers to the unrestricted impact of the Renaissance, with its dangerous proclivities towards paganism and Protestantism. The path she had chosen for herself led from the Middle Ages straight to the Counter-Reformation, and she would not tolerate for long any influences likely to deflect her from that course.

ECONOMIC AND SOCIAL CONDITIONS

That course had been set by Castile, by far the stronger of the associated kingdoms. The Crown of Aragon appears to have had at that time only about one-third of the territory, and one-sixth or one-seventh the population, of her Castilian partner.[11] The mercantile vigour which had brought her prosperity and influence in the Middle Ages had been sapped by a number of setbacks: the savage outbreaks of plague in the fourteenth century, with their train of peasant risings and civil war, the fall of Constantinople and the rise of Turkish naval power, the commercial rivalry of the Genoese, and finally the stimulus given to the Atlantic ports and sea-routes by the discovery of America. Castile, on the other hand, with its population of between six and seven million, was astir with new life. Astir in a very real sense; the Court itself, the country's administrative and social nerve-centre, was constantly on the move between the great cities such as Valladolid, Burgos, Segovia, Cordova and Granada, for it was not until the latter half of the sixteenth century that a permanent capital was established at Madrid. Commercial life revolved around the great annual fairs, the most famous of which was held at Medina del Campo. But already streams of soldiers, traders and adventurers of all sorts were making their way towards Seville, soon to emerge as the country's commercial metropolis, thanks to its monopoly of trade with the New World and the many-sided activities of the Casa de Contratación set up in 1503 as a great School of Navigation and clearing house for the despatch of fleets, cargoes and emigrants to the Indies.

This was also the time when the value of Castile's sheep and wool trade steadily increased. There was a seasonal migration of the vast flocks of sheep, as many as two or three million in number, between their winter pastures in the north and their summer pastures in the south, four hundred miles or more away. The sweeping uplands of Castile, with their poor soil and dry climate, had always been more suited to grazing than to cultivatio 1, and the emphasis on stock raising had been intensified by the centuries of warfare against the Moor, when wealth was reckoned in flocks and herds. After the introduction, around 1300, of the merino sheep, the quality of Spanish wool showed a marked improvement. A nation-wide association of sheepowners known as the *Mesta* was formed and received all manner of privileges and protection from the Crown, which drew upon its increasing wealth for urgently needed taxes and loans. But the favour shown to the Mesta led inevitably to conflict between the pastoral and agricultural interests, to the detriment of the latter. The Crown even went so far as to decree that 'all land on which the migrant flocks had even once been pastured was reserved in perpetuity for pasturage and could not be put to any other uses by its owner. This meant that great tracts of land in Andalusia and Estremadura were deprived of all chance of agricultural development and subjected to the whim of the sheepowners.'[12] Spain was to pay dearly for this neglect of agriculture, for it proved a basic cause of her decline.

Spain's booming wool-trade brought her many advantages. Not only did it provide the Crown with a steady source of revenue, but through the *Consulado* set up in Burgos on the pattern of the *consolat de la mar* in the medieval Kingdom of Aragon, important trade links were developed with Flanders which anticipated the political links which were to follow when both countries came under the rule of Charles V, the Holy Roman Emperor. Moreover, since sheep-raising requires less labour than agriculture, Castile could use the surplus manpower for her tercios in Europe and for the conquest and colonization of the New World. The conquistadors were primarily men of this pastoral-military breed, even the meanest of whom looked to make their fortune by force of arms and through the spoils of war rather than by themselves tilling the soil of the newly won lands. Nevertheless, European plants, livestock and agricultural techniques were quickly introduced into the colonies and for a few decades the Crown encouraged a relative freedom of trade in which not only the Aragonese, but also the Emperor's other European subjects were allowed some share. But monopolist views came to prevail. The colonies were not allowed to produce commodities which might harm the mother country's chief exports; therefore Peru's recently planted vineyards and olive groves were ordered to be destroyed lest those of Andalusia should suffer from their competition. Furthermore, all trade with the New World was to be channelled through Seville, which thus came to enjoy nearly two centuries of commercial monopoly.

Though anxious to protect her markets in the New World, Spain was chiefly concerned with securing what she valued most: plentiful supplies of gold and silver with which to pay her armies and cover the mounting costs of her imperial responsibilities. The Indies poured forth their treasure in profusion, but never in quantities sufficient for the insatiable royal appetite. First came a trickle of gold from the Antilles, then the spoils of the Aztecs and the still more fabulous plunder of the Incas. New mines were sought for and exploited, culminating in the stupendous discovery of the silver-hill of Potosí, high up in the Bolivian Andes. This bullion, of which the Crown continued to receive her royal fifth, was sent in the heavily defended treasure-fleets which sailed to Spain twice every year. Its effect soon began to make itself felt on the economy of Castile. Inflation set in, spurred still further by the failure of agriculture to feed Castile's growing population and at the same time supply the needs of her colonies. In the course of the sixteenth century, prices appear to have risen by 400 per cent.

Those who were hardest hit by the rising cost of living were the poorest section of the population on whom the main brunt of taxation already fell. Even in the period of imperial greatness, when the lucky few might make their fortunes in the New World, the poor were never safe for long from the spectre of starvation. In years of bad harvest, heavy imports of foreign grain barely sufficed to stave off famine and swarms of hungry vagrants thronged the highways. Spain, a land of the very rich and the very poor, saw the former grow richer and the latter even poorer. This was largely due to the traditional exemption from taxation enjoyed by all those of noble birth, and to the *mayor-azgo* system of handing down entailed estates to the eldest son. As these estates were constantly augmented through marriage, buying up the lands of hard-pressed small farmers, and in other ways, there was a consequent trend towards the concentration of more and more land among a few landholders. It is estimated that 97 per cent of the soil of Castile came to be owned by 2 per cent of the population, over half of this area being the property of a handful of great families.[13] Twenty-five of the latter, the cream of the aristocracy, had the rank of Grandees and a number of valued but mostly empty privileges such as the right to remain covered in the presence of the King and to be addressed by him as 'cousin'. Whilst respecting their social pre-eminence, it was the Crown's prudent policy to exclude the Gran-dees as far as possible from political power, and to choose most of its advisers and officials from amongst *letrados*, churchmen, younger sons of the nobility, and from the *hidalgos* who formed its lower strata. From the two latter groups came many of Spain's leading commanders and conquistadors, such as Gonzalo de Córdoba and Cortés.

Many hidalgos, however, despite their exemption from taxation, remained poor and had to pinch and scheme in order to maintain the state to which they felt themselves entitled, as we know from the portrait of his impecunious master drawn by the servant-boy in the first and most attractive of the picaresque novels, *Lazarillo de Tormes*, and by Cervantes' description of Don Quixote, whose 'diet consisted more of beef than of mutton; and with minced meat on most nights, lentils on Fridays, griefs and groans on Saturdays and a pigeon extraordinary on Sundays, he consumed three quarters of his revenue; the rest was laid out in a plush coat, velvet breeches, with slippers of the same, for holidays; and a suit of the very best homespun cloth, which he bestowed on himself for working days.'

Don Quixote's obsession with sallying out into the world in quest of fantastic adventures and the famished hidalgo's dread of losing caste by honest toil were deformations of a once valid ideal. In the centuries of the Reconquista, the heroic virtues of courage, tenacity, and military prowess were paramount; so were the chivalric ideals – though often lightly regarded in practice – of loyalty, justice and the defence of the oppressed. The exercise of these virtues might well be crowned with fame and fortune, as every conquistador still hoped. All were avid readers – as were such heroic saints as St Ignatius Loyola and Santa Teresa – of the miraculous exploits of Amadís de Gaula or other heroes in the popular books of chivalry. Bernal Diaz recalls that as he and his companions gazed for the first time on Montezuma's fabulous capital, 'we were all struck with amazement and exclaimed that the towers, temples and lakes seemed like the enchantments we read of in *Amadís*'.[14]

In time, the supply of Moors or Indians to be conquered, and of new lands to be won, ran out, and the heroic ideal turned in upon itself and grew sterile. The concern with honour – a man's pride in his personal integrity and achievements – degenerated into a concern for punctilio and mere reputation. The extreme to which this process was later carried is mirrored in the dramas of Calderón, many of which deal with the husband's right to avenge himself for a real, or even an imagined, slur on his honour by personally contriving the death of his wife and her gallant. Such cases occurred not only on the stage but in real life, as we learn from a record of 1637: 'On Maundy Thursday, Miguel Pérez de las Navas, royal notary, having waited for the day when his wife had made confession and communicated, assumed the functions of executioner, and after begging her forgiveness, strangled her in their home, all on account of certain trivial suspicions of infidelity.'[15] The code of honour, noble and exemplary in its origins, had become perverted into the antithesis of common humanity and Christian ethics.

The profession of Catholic faith – an essential feature of medieval chivalry – suffered a similar distortion. To take pride in being a Christian, when Spain was overrun with Jews and Moslems, was one thing; to pride oneself on being an 'old Christian', and hence to despise the descendants of those Jews and Moslems who had been received into their church, was quite another. Faith was contaminated

67

by racialism; *limpieza de sangre* – purity of blood – became a fetish. Entry into the military orders, certain of the religious orders, cathedral chapters, university institutions, and even the guilds of merchants and craftsmen, was closed against those who could not show a spotless pedigree. The common people, who had no pedigrees anyway, and had been less affected by intermarriage, were equally, if not more, ready to pride themselves on being 'old Christians'. Limpieza de sangre thus became, as it were, the poor man's 'honour'. Even Sancho could boast; 'I am one of your old Christians, and that is enough to qualify me to be an earl'. But if Sancho, infected by the megalomania of his master, the Knight, dreamed of one day being made the governor of an island, the mass of the common people remained bound to the soil and preserved the old virtues of the race as their country sank into decline. Amongst them, if anywhere, the old concept of honour as the hard core of a man's personal integrity still lived on, as we find it embodied in the peasant-hero of Calderón's fine play, *El Alcalde de Zalamea*.

THE EMPEROR CHARLES V

The death of King Ferdinand in 1516 opened a new and unexpected chapter in Spanish history. When Isabel had died, twelve years before, the Crown of Castile had passed to their mentally unbalanced daughter Juana and her husband, Philip of Burgundy. But Philip succumbed to a fever shortly afterwards, leaving his anguished widow, henceforth to be known as Juana the Mad, manifestly incapable of governing. Their sixteen-year-old son Charles, totally ignorant of Spain and dependent on his Flemish advisers, thus inherited the Crowns of Castile and Aragon, in addition to his father's possessions of the Netherlands and the Franche-Comté. His election, three years later, to be Holy Roman Emperor, made him the most powerful ruler in Europe since Charlemagne. But Charles' Spanish subjects, who feared that this honour would cause them to see less of the king but more of the tax-collector, made no secret of their displeasure. The remarkable thing is that this insipid Flemish youth became, as the great Emperor Charles V, deeply attached to Spain, though his European preoccupations kept him out of the country for all but sixteen out of the forty years of his reign, whilst Spain, so loath at first to enter the wider European stage, came to take pride and relish in her imperial role.[16] During the reign of Charles V her history, and that of Europe, are one. At first there was strong protest at the new order of things, with the cities feeling particularly threatened. They feared the growing power of the Crown and the new taxes which were levied for imperial needs. The city revolts were hampered by local rivalries and lack of common objectives. In Castile, where many nobles at first supported, or at least did not oppose, it, the rising gradually acquired overtones of more radical, social protest. In Valencia, where it developed more or less independently and is known as the revolt of the *germanías* or brotherhoods, it was from the outset mainly a movement of the common people against the privileged nobility.

As soon as Charles had left Spain to attend to affairs in North Europe, there was general discontent among the leading cities of Castile. People in the streets chanted 'Long live the King – and death to his evil councillors'. Toledo and other towns set up communes, raised militia, and sent delegates to a *Junta Santa* at Avila. When imperialist troops, in an attempt to reassert their authority, set fire to Medina del Campo and burned its well-stocked warehouses to the ground, the mood of defiance and indignation only deepened. Gradually disagreements developed in the rebel ranks. Many of the nobles returned to their allegiance, and a rebel body, more radical than the Junta Santa, passed a resolution declaring that 'henceforth the war was against grandees, *caballeros*, and other enemies of the realm, and against their properties and palaces to be waged with fire and sack and blood'.[17] Without the support of these same caballeros the rebels were no match militarily for the imperialist forces and they were routed at Villalar.

By the time Charles returned to Spain in 1522, Castile – and Aragon a few months later – were pacified and he could grant a general pardon to all except the ringleaders. The bid to set up the power of the communes against the apparatus of royal absolutism had failed. Even though this marked the decline of the cities as a political factor and left a legacy of faction and bitterness, the gesture

69

had not been altogether vain. Charles learned from it an important lesson in his development as a ruler – the need to respect the will and traditions of his Spanish subjects. The Cortes continued to meet at intervals throughout his reign, and if they made no further serious attempt to challenge the royal authority, Charles at least never disregarded them so blatantly as Henry VIII of England and Francis I of France disregarded their parliaments.

The defeat of the *Comuneros* marked a turning point in the destiny of Spain. Charles' victory represented 'the momentary triumph of Europe over Castile' and 'the definitive establishment of an alien dy׳ nasty with an alien programme which threatened to submerge Castile in the larger entity of a universal Empire.'[18] Spain was henceforth to devote her resources to the Emperor's threefold struggle: against the Turkish power in North Africa and the Mediterranean; against France, particularly in Italy, where the Duchy of Milan commanded the imperial lines of communication between the Kingdom of Naples and his German possessions; against German princes in their striv׳ ings for political independence. In the ebb and flow of this incessant campaigning, at the diplomats' conference׳table and the theologians' interminable debates at Trent, Spain made the Emperor's cause her own and gave of her best. And at last the Emperor, worn down by the burden of all this grandeur, shifted it to his son's shoulders and withdrew to end his days in Castile which had become the soul of his imperial endeavours.

There was also the burden of the vast, sprawling, half׳tamed empire of the New World. If Charles' preoccupations in Europe seem remote enough from those of our own times, the impact upon primi׳ tive peoples of a more civilized and technologically advanced nation raised problems which are still very much with us today. The empire of the New World was an enterprise of adventurous individuals which the Crown needed to sanction, control, and institutionalize. It set about the task in no merely pragmatic or opportunist spirit, but with a real concern for the juridical, ethical and theological prin׳ ciples involved – a fruitful interplay of thought and action, which has been characteristic of Spanish life at its best. The nation at large took part in the great debate; colonists, officials, friars, lawyers and theologians argued about the ethics of the Conquista, the nature of the Indians and the rights of Spain to wage war and exercise sovereignty. Were the Indians 'natural slaves', as the eminent Aristotelian Ginés de Sepúlveda affirmed, an irremediably inferior race destined to live subordinate to the white conquerors? Or were they, in the words of Friar Bartolomé de las Casas, ex-conquistador turned passionate champion of the natives, 'uncultivated soil that readily brings forth weeds and thorns, but has within it such natural virtues that by labour and cultivation may be made to yield sound and beneficial fruit'? In 1550 Charles summoned a council of leading jurists and theologians to Valladolid to consider and advise him on these weighty issues. After years of passionate debate and pains-taking study, the Council dispersed without reaching any con-clusive findings, though each side claimed the victory. Even though Las Casas still has his opponents, his humanism accords more nearly with our own way of thinking. At all events, the Crown was deeply influenced by the enlightened views of such men as Las Casas, and if royal provisions were often nullified by interested parties on the spot, the great corpus of legislation comprised in the Laws of the Indies remains an abiding monument to the Crown's concern for Spain's Indian subjects. There is much truth in the claim that no other nation made so continuous or so passionate an attempt to discover what was the just treatment for the native peoples under its jurisdiction'.[19]

THE REIGN OF PHILIP II

The inheritance which Philip received from his father was com-pounded of old problems and new opportunities. The problems were the perennial threat posed by Islam, now represented by the Ottoman Empire, the Barbary pirates and Spain's own dissident Morisco subjects; the rising nationalism of the Netherlands now greatly influenced by Lutheranism; France, always alert to make common cause with Spain's Moslem or Dutch enemies, and even at times in danger of herself slipping into Protestantism. Philip had inherited a more manageable empire, now composed of three inter-related units: the New World, Spain and Italy, and the Netherlands together with, it was hoped, after Philip's marriage to Mary Tudor, England. The strategy of territorial accession through dynastic unions was also in time to secure for Philip the reversion of Portugal, thus rounding off the political unity of the whole Iberian peninsula. To these problems and opportunities Philip addressed himself with industry and high seriousness. Freed from his father's cosmopolitan preoccupations, he could devote himself wholly to furthering Spain's national interests and defending the cause of Catholicism. If his policies sometimes set him at odds with the Papacy, this was only because Philip considered religion too serious a matter to be left to the Pope.

In facing the threat from Islam, Pope and King could, at all events, make common cause. For Spain, the threat was internal as well as external. We have seen how after an initial period of tolerance, the Crown had imposed on the conquered Moors a choice between emigration or conversion. Most had opted for the latter, but after half a century of nominal Christianity, the Moriscos still remained obstinately attached to their ancestral ways and many continued to observe Moslem rites in secret. In 1567, Philip attempted to end this once and for all by issuing a decree requiring the renunciation of all Moslem practices, including the use of Arabic books and the Arabic tongue. This resulted in a fresh rising in Granada and the Alpujarras, in the course of which churches were desecrated and Christians murdered. Peace was restored only after a harsh campaign commanded by Philip's youthful half-brother, Don Juan of Austria, and the deportation of all Moslems from the province of Granada into other parts of Spain. These drastic measures were justified by the threat posed by a dissident Moslem population inviting intervention by their co-religionists abroad. Some hundreds of volunteers had come from Algiers to help rebels in the Alpujarras, and plans for a full-scale invasion had been considered by the Ottoman Sultan but turned down in favour of an attack against Venetian possessions. When, therefore, Pope Pius V urged the formation of an anti-Ottoman Holy Alliance between Spain, Venice and the Papacy, Philip readily consented. Spanish troops under the command of Don Juan of Austria played a major part in the great battle of Lepanto in which the bulk of the Turkish fleet was destroyed by the Alliance;

a victory described by Cervantes, who himself fought and was wounded there, as 'the most memorable occasion that either past or present ages beheld, or the future can hope to see'. Memorable as Lepanto proved to be, it was not the end of Spain's long struggle with Islam, which was to come in the following reign with the expulsion from Spain of the Moors of Valencia and all other parts of Spain.

A less painful measure in the unification of the peninsula was the reversion to Philip of the Portuguese throne. His chance came in 1578, when his cousin, the impetuous young King Sebastian, per-ished in a disastrous African crusade. Philip had a good claim to the succession through his mother, daughter of King Manuel of Portu-gal. Acting with uncharacteristic speed, Philip sent a Castilian army into Portugal to enforce his claim. Though the Portuguese people remained bitterly anti-Spanish, those nobles who had sur-vived the African disaster were mostly won over, whilst banking and mercantile circles in Lisbon saw that they had much to gain from the Castilian connection. Philip used his victory with a re-straint which justified his sobriquet of El Rey Prudente. The liberties and institutions of Portugal remained intact, as had those of Aragon on uniting with Castile a century earlier. No Castilians were per-mitted to hold office in Portugal, whilst the latter continued to administer her overseas possessions and to enjoy a monopoly of trade with them. Nevertheless, union with Portugal brought Spain some solid gains. She could now use Portugal's invaluable fleets and harbours in her struggle against the rebellious Dutch, and against England, the new Atlantic power which was beginning to threaten her communications in the Channel and to challenge Spanish hegemony in the New World.

The situation in the Netherlands had been deteriorating since 1560. To deal with it Philip had to choose between a policy of ruthless repression or the more conciliatory approach advocated by the moderates at court. Protestantism continued to gain in the northern provinces, and Philip was more then ever convinced that heretic spelled rebel. He despatched the Duke of Alba with instruc-tions to extirpate it mercilessly. After seven years of terror, this 'hard line' policy proved a failure, and Alba was replaced by a more

moderate governor, who died soon after his arrival in the Netherlands. The unpaid Spanish troops sacked Antwerp, and the whole
Netherlands was united in a fresh outburst of hatred against Spanish
misrule. Philip then sent Don Juan of Austria whom neither his
own temperament nor the mood of the rebels permitted to play the
role of conciliator. Only after the death of Don Juan and the appointment of the Duke of Parma, an able diplomat and perhaps the
greatest strategist of his day, did Philip's prospects improve. Elsewhere, events were moving in his favour, for the feud with the powerful Guise family in France had been healed. It remained only to
consolidate Spain's position by the conquest of England which,
in addition to stepping up attacks on Spanish possessions in the New
World, had been steadily increasing its aid to the Dutch rebels.
Philip was confident that once Parma's army had been conveyed
across the Channel, the issue could be safely left to the seasoned tercios
and the military genius of their commander. The destruction in 1588
of the Invincible Armada despatched to effect this grand design
proved indeed the momentous event for the destiny of England that
every school-child is taught to believe.

We can be less sure about the traditional picture of Philip as a
fanatical, gloomy and bloodthirsty tyrant – the monster of the Escurial
spinning plots for the destruction of individual liberties and national
independence throughout the world. Fanatical he certainly was in
the strength of his religious convictions, his equating of Catholic
with Spanish interests, of heresy with rebellion; but his sense of being
God's chosen instrument on earth also inspired him with a genuine
concern for social justice and the rights of the humblest of his subjects. He was stoical in his endurance of the numerous misfortunes,
whether public or private, which befell him. The sunnier side of his
temperament shines out from the delightful and affectionate letters
which he wrote to his young daughters. One of the bitterest tragedies
of his life was the pathological viciousness and incapacity of his only
son, Don Carlos, whom he was eventually compelled to place under
restraint. When that unfortunate prince died shortly afterwards, the
King's enemies asserted that it was at his father's command. These
and other calumnies were spread abroad by the King's ex-secretary,

Antonio Pérez, whose defection was the greatest political scandal of the day. At times of crisis Philip acted with severity, but his rule was not generally oppressive. His subjects could complain not so much of its tyranny as of its cumbrous bureaucracy. Philip, obsessed with the responsibilities of his high office, strove to take every detail of state administration onto his own shoulders. He commented in his own hand on the innumerable memoranda placed before him by his secretaries and councils, taking every decision himself, whether relating to the engaging of a footman or the conclusion of a treaty. At the end of his reign in 1598, the pulse of empire beat ever more faintly through the clogged arteries of the Escurial.

ART, RELIGION AND LITERATURE

The palace of the Escurial was the affirmation of the spirit of the Counter-Reformation, Italian Renaissance disciplined by the austerity of Castile. It was designed as something more than a royal residence and superministry – to serve as a mausoleum for his family and himself, and as a monastery for the Hieronymite monks. It also served to house the library and the paintings which Philip collected or commissioned from all parts of Europe. Amongst the artists who hoped to win the favour of the royal patron was a young Greek trained in Italy whom his contemporaries knew as El Greco. The one painting which Philip commissioned from him won little favour. The elongated, distorted forms, the two-dimensional Byzantine composition, the eerie light and vivid colours were found strange and disturbing. But El Greco's work struck a responsive chord in the fervently pious hearts of priests and monks, whose patronage enabled him to make his home and a good living in Toledo, the ecclesiastical capital of the country. In this climate, where Christian, Jewish and Moslem influences had met and mingled, El Greco's unique genius flowered, and it is here, in the sixteenth-century house now converted into a museum, and on the walls of the churches where they were first commissioned, that his paintings still make their greatest impact. To stand in San Tomé before the *Burial of Count Orgaz* is to glimpse into the spirit of Spain's great age. Here, in the grandiose composition of this extraordinary work, the terrestrial and the celestial worlds are fused into one. St Stephen and St Augustine have joined the canons of Toledo Cathedral to bear up the body of the pious nobleman. Behind them stand a row of hidalgos in their ruffs and black suits, each grave face a portrait of some friend or patron of the painter, whilst high above them, in the presence of the Virgin Mary and the angelic host, God Almighty receives the soul which has passed through death into true life.

If El Greco is the most powerfully idiosyncratic of Spanish painters, Velásquez is the most European. The first painted for the Church, the second for the Court. El Greco's figures seem to be extruded, like ectoplasm, from his own mind; those of Velásquez are based on precise observation of nature and the meticulous practice of his early years, to which we owe the scenes from common life in the *bodegón*, or 'kitchen sink', style of the day. This native realism was refined by the constant study of the Italian masters and the influence of Rubens, who visited the Spanish court on a diplomatic mission, and by a tireless curiosity in exploring the complexities of light and space. The technical virtuosity which he achieved in this field is revealed in his famous picture *Las Meninas* where we find ourselves watching, in an astonishing three-dimensional composition, the little fair-haired infanta in her immense farthingale surrounded by her maids-in-waiting, with a court dwarf and a drowsy mastiff in the foreground, whilst the artist stands at his easel with up-lifted brush and the King himself surveys the scene from a doorway in the background. Apart from an occasional set-piece like the *Surrender of Breda* or the exquisite reclining nude of *The Toilet of Venus* – a subject normally frowned upon by the Inquisition – Velásquez worked mainly on portraits. And what a gallery they present!

Velásquez, who was appointed chief painter to the royal family in 1623, was seldom called upon to treat religious themes, but when he did so, his paintings have a moving and manly quality about them which, like all his work, is utterly free from sentimentality. The latter was a taint from which not all his contemporaries escaped, which is not surprising when we recall the norms prescribed by the Inquisition, as laid down in the treatise on the art of painting written by his father-in-law, Pacheco. These required that the Virgin should be depicted 'in the flower of her age, from twelve to thirteen years old, with sweet grave eyes, a nose and mouth of the most perfect hue'. Hence the cloying sweetness of many of the *Purísimas* of Murillo, an artist who also painted many robust portraits and scenes from popular life but was held in most esteem for his numerous versions of the Immaculate Conception. Other painters, instead of reserving their realistic bent for pictures of the bodegón type, brought it to bear on their treatment of religious themes. Ribalta, and particularly Ribera, who lived in Naples and learned from Caravaggio the dramatic effects to be obtained from the strong contrasts of light and deep shadow, excel in depicting the pain-racked bodies of saints, hermits and martyrs. But the artist whose work combines the most consummate mastery of realistic treatment with intensity of religious feeling is the Estremaduran Zurbarán. As a painter of still-life he has few equals. Zurbarán brings the same miraculous talent for conveying the tactile quality of things to his rendering of the stiff white and brown habits of his monks, the earthy Spanish peasant faces through which shines forth the fervour of their inner faith. No one has ever painted monks as Zurbarán painted them, nor evoked more convincingly the moments of ecstasy which illuminated the cloistered life.

The naturalistic, and often harrowing, treatment of religious themes in painting and sculpture – for the polychrome carvings of Berreguete and Juan de Juni can be almost unbearably life-like in their anguish – was encouraged by the Church as a means of inciting the observer to penitence and devotion. This is clearly prescribed in the *Spiritual Exercises* of St Ignatius Loyola, which, as a training manual for the conquest of the world for God through the conquest of the self, must surely rank as one of the most influential books ever written. In the personality of Ignatius, the Basque hidalgo turned saint, we find blended the two strands of Spain's religious genius – the militant aspect, which we have called the spirit of Santiago Matamoros, and the contemplative aspect, which was to reach fullest expression in the lives of the great mystics. St Ignatius was convalescing painfully from a war wound which the surgeons feared would prove fatal, 'and since he was a great reader of those vain and worldly books called Romances of Chivalry, he asked to be given some with which to pass away the time; but in that house there happened to be none of such as he was wont to read, so they gave him instead *Vita Christi* and a book of the lives of saints, written in the vulgar tongue'.[20] He was moved by his reading to emulate the heroic sufferings of the saints, and after keeping all night vigil before the shrine of Our Lady of Montserrat Ignatius embarked on the spiritual pilgrimage which was to culminate in the founding of the Company of Jesus. Binding himself and his companions with a special vow of obedience to the Pope, the Jesuits became the great bastion of orthodoxy, the shock-troops of the Counter-Reformation.

The richness and variety of Spanish mystical writings bear witness to the prevailing craving for spiritual perfection which was no less intense in that extraordinary age than the hunger for worldly fame and fortune. Much of the pious literature is of a devotional and didactic character which has little appeal today, though the works of probably its greatest exponent, Friar Luis de Granada, are still read for the superb sweep and balance of his prose. Our interest is drawn today primarily to those works which were never conceived as litera-ture but which were written on the instructions of a worried con-fessor anxious to determine whether the abnormal experiences of his penitent were of God or the Devil.[21] Some of the greatest mystics of the age, like St Peter of Alcántara, whom St Teresa described as so old and gnarled with his mortifications that his body seemed 'all made of the roots of trees', left only the slightest written records of their experi-ences. St Teresa herself wrote her *Life* at the behest of her confessor, and her other works as a spiritual guide for her nuns. In vigorous, vivid prose she describes as clearly as possible in human terms the successive stages through which the soul passes in its ascent to God. Yet she never – and this is a measure of her Spanishness – loses touch with reality. For the saint, reality has an extra spiritual dimension, and when St Teresa writes that 'God walks amongst the pots and pans', she is recording a direct and almost literal experience.

Mystics may be the most practical of people. Teresa of Avila led a full and active life, and founded seventeen convents in the space of twenty years. In her zeal to reform the Carmelite Order, she was assisted by a young friar, St John of the Cross, who incurred the wrath of his more worldly brethren and was imprisoned by them in Toledo. There, in the gloom of his prison cell, his spiritual ecstasies blossomed. His beautiful poem generally known as *La Noche Oscura* is both an allegory of the soul's flight through the dark night of renunciation towards union with the divine Beloved, and an allusion to his own escape from prison to rejoin his companions of the Reform.[22] His poetry has a unique passionate quality of its own. It is the sort of poetry which, as Gerald Brenan says, 'has never been written in Spain to women; tenderness, abandon, delight were reserved for religious occasions.'[23]

Another outstanding poet whose work was impregnated with strong mystical feeling and who suffered a spell of imprisonment through the malice of his enemies was the Augustinian friar and Professor at Salamanca University, Luis de León. He was a man of ardent temperament whose agitated life contrasts with the Platonic serenity of his verse. The mystic union to which Friar Luis aspires seems to be one of cosmic comprehension, where 'transformed into radiant light, I shall behold, at once separate and in union, what is and what has been, the secret fount of all being'. Though steeped in the classics, Luis de León enriched his work with the new forms and metres introduced from Italy by Garcilaso de la Vega, the most brilliant secular poet of the day, and his friend Juan Boscán. The latter also published an excellent Spanish version of Castiglione's famous book *The Courtier* which went through fourteen editions before the end of the century. Another book much read in Spain from the middle of the century was Montemayor's *Diana*, which started the vogue of the pastoral novel. In the conversation of his love-sick nymphs and swains we catch an echo of the pervasive neo-platonism and recognize in the Arcadian groves the stylized landscape described in Luis de León's great prose work, *Names of Christ*.

In contrast both to the literature of mysticism and to that of escapism, as represented by the pastoral novel and the romances of chivalry, we find another very different and distinctively Spanish genre developing – the picaresque novel.[24] The rogue or *pícaro* is spurred on by hunger, as the conquistador is driven by his craving for fame and fortune and the mystic by his vision of God. His life-story is a series of adventures, generally sordid and scurrilous, in search of the next meal. The pícaro is no revolutionary or rebel against society; he applies all his ingenuity and roguery to securing a place in it as it is, however menial. There is a strong autobiographical element in most picaresque novels. But if we would look for literary precedents for the genre we may perhaps find them in a unique and unclassifiable masterpiece published anonymously at the end of the fifteenth century and generally known, after its central character, as *La Celestina*. In this cruder and more violent Romeo and Juliet tale interest centres less on the passion of the young couple than on the pullulating underworld dominated by the scheming, wheedling old bawd and procuress, Celestina, who brings the lovers together and finally perishes herself in their tragedy.

La Celestina, though styled a tragi-comedy and cast in dramatic form, was intended to be read rather than acted. Almost another century was to elapse before the vogue for the theatre set in and there appeared a 'prodigy of nature' to feed the insatiable popular appetite with a succession of fast-moving plays known as the *comedias de capa y espada*. In Lope de Vega, the copious and exuberant inventiveness of the age reaches its fullest expression. There survive some 500 of his plays, probably about a third of his dramatic output, to say nothing of his two long novels and a vast body of poetry. Nor did these Herculean literary labours divert Lope from the business of living. He threw himself with equal zest into every sort of business and social activity, tumultuous love affairs, military adventures and religious practices. He volunteered for, and survived the defeat of, the Armada. These experiences, and particularly the insight he gained into the passions and stratagems of love, were transmuted with zest, gaiety and inimitable lyrical grace into his plays. They are crammed with incidents, in every type of setting, with characters delineated by a few bold strokes – kings and peasants, pícaros and saints, ladies of quality and intriguing bawds, with the *gracioso's* clowning to set off the high drama, and sometimes whole communities, such as the village of Fuenteovejuna in the famous play of that name, to serve as a collective hero. It is an immensely varied and vital world, passing quickly from comedy to tragedy and if it sometimes offends our taste by the implausibility of the plot and its ready recourse to the supernatural, we must remember that the Spaniards of that day viewed the events of even the most worldly life *sub specie aeternitatis*. They saw nothing surprising in the intervention of angels or demons; moreover, they understood that, if the play culminated in the death of an apparently blameless hero or heroine, there would assuredly follow a final act enacted, not on the stage, but in paradise, to ensure the happy ending of the salvation of an immortal soul. Thus, though we recognize in Lope's theatre many features of our own Elizabethan drama, the underlying theological and social assumptions may escape us. The plays of 'honour', in which the offended male takes vengeance into his own hands, we may find particularly hard to stomach.[25]

Two other dramatists deserve special note; Guillén de Castro and the Mercedarian friar who wrote under the name of Tirso de Molina. The first is remembered chiefly for his spirited play which drew freely on the popular romances dealing with the exploits of the Cid. Tirso heightened the dramatic interest of this legendary material by depicting the Cid as in love with the woman whose father he was called upon to slay in revenge for an affront to family honour. This theme aroused the interest of the French dramatist Corneille, who developed it still further in his famous play *Le Cid*. Tirso de Molina is the creator of a figure whose appeal to the poetic imagination has been even stronger and more universal. In the *Burlador de Sevilla* we see Don Juan Tenorio, in a lightning campaign of seduction and insolent trickery, precisely in the field which is most hedged around by principles of 'honour' and the sanctity of the marriage bond, fulfilling what we are told is the universal secret ambition: 'this Spaniard is authorized to do just whatever he pleases'. Other ages and societies have produced their own version of this perennially fascinating figure. Molière has given us his courtly cad, Byron his charming and unprincipled young man falling for every attractive woman, Mozart his melodious Don Giovanni, and a later Spanish dramatist, Zorrilla, his romantic hero in quest of the ideal woman who finally redeems him by the force and purity of her love.

The Cid, Don Juan – there is yet another and greater arche-
typal figure which we owe to Spain – Don Quixote de la Mancha.
We have already met the Castilian hidalgo – proud, impecunious,
dreaming of fame; but Cervantes' hero has had his head turned
through reading too many romances of chivalry. Convinced that
he was 'born into this iron age to restore the Age of Gold', Don
Quixote sets off on his nag, Rosinante, across the desolate plains
of La Mancha to exercise his calling as Knight Errant and to
win imperishable renown through the prodigies of his valour. His
obsession leads him to mistake an inn for a castle, a village wench for
his peerless Dulcinea, a windmill for a giant, a flock of sheep for a
hostile army, and a barber's basin for Membrino's famous helmet.
After innumerable ludicrous and painful encounters, a disillusioned
Don Quixote returns home. An illiterate villager, Sancho Panza,
accompanies him, and the contrast between the crazed but noble-
minded knight and his earthy squire, endlessly discussing their
adventures and life in general, is one of the delights of the book; and
where else but in Spain could one find a relationship between master
and man at once so intimate and yet of such mutual respect? The
story has sometimes been taken as an allegory of the Spanish nation,
led on by delusions of fame and grandeur into ignoring the harsh
realities which eventually bring it to ruin. In its vast range Cervantes'
masterpiece includes within itself the substance of all other books
written about Spain. It is natural that his countrymen should return
to it again and again for a deeper understanding of themselves and
the genius of their land.

Three other names are great enough to be mentioned in the same
breath as Cervantes: Calderón, Góngora and Quevedo. Calderón
de la Barca succeeded Lope as the foremost playwright of his day. An
accomplished author of *capa y espada* comedies and the musical
productions known as *zarzuelas*, Calderón also excelled in the
composition of *autos sacramentales* – religious plays intended to cele-
brate the mystery of the Eucharist at the feast of Corpus Christi –
and exploited to the full the dramatic possibilities of the drama of
'honour'. One of his works, *The Mayor of Zalamea*, treats this latter
theme in an unusual way, since it portrays the honour not of a

hidalgo but of a peasant, who justifies his execution of a tyrannous royal official with the famous lines:

To the King we owe life and property; but honour is the patrimony of the soul, and the soul belongs to God alone.

Calderón's best known play is *Life is a Dream*, an allegory of human destiny and enquiry into the nature of reality. Like Calderón's other dramas, it is written in verse of Miltonic sweep and magnificence which shows the influence of Góngora, the greatest poetic genius of the day. Góngora evolved a completely new baroque style of writing known as *culteranismo*, in which he composed a vast unfinished poem known as the *Solitudes*. Because of its elaborate metaphors and its dense and complex meaning, this poem is too often impenetrable except for the specialist.[26] In Góngora's day, culteranismo had its passionate partisans and its no less fervent enemies. Amongst the latter was the brilliant satirist Quevedo, whose many works include the extraordinary *Sueños* or Dreams, which have been described as 'visions of the Day of Judgment, Hell and the Kingdom of Death which, starting off from some point of profound melancholy, break down into satire, macabre buffoonery and a sort of phantasmagoric nonsense'.[27] The savage pessimism of Quevedo stems not only from the imprisonment of an acute mind and ardent temperament in a deformed body, but from the *Zeitgeist* of an age now manifestly in decay. Quevedo is forever looking back to the days of Spain's greatness, pouring out his spleen against Jews, Moors and foreigners in general and his scorn for attempts to rebuild the country's industry and commerce and cut down its military commitments. He defends the Inquisition and champions St James the Moorslayer against the proposal to have St Teresa raised to be co-patron of Spain. In a word, Quevedo is the most intransigent of reactionaries. Even though he vociferously opposed all liberal remedies, he at least realized, with passionate and anguished intensity, that his country was slipping into inexorable decline.

1 *The Bulls of Guisando,*
pre-Roman stone carvings
in a field near Avila.

2 This Roman aqueduct
near Tarragona is one of
the many fine monuments
of the Roman occupation
which left a deep impress on
the landscape and
civilization of Spain.

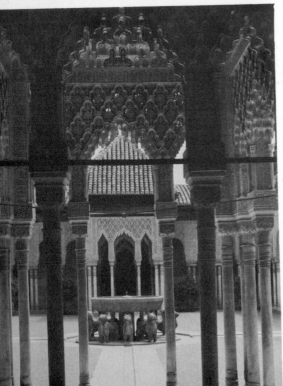

3 The Cathedral, formerly the great mosque, of Cordova, capital of Spain after the Moslem conquest. 4 The Courtyard of the Lions in the Alhambra, Granada, is a masterpiece of late Islamic-Spanish art. Granada held out against the Christians until the year Columbus discovered America. 5 *The Cid* (below), an old woodcut depicting Rodrigo Díaz de Vivar, hero of the famous Spanish epic poem. 6 The castle at Segovia, where Isabel the Catholic was proclaimed Queen of Castile in 1474. 7 The Cathedral at Santiago de Compostela (far right). The shrine, traditionally held to mark the tomb of St James, became a great centre of European pilgrimage. 8 (Opposite below) Santiago Matamoros, St James the Moorslayer, was adopted by the Christians as their patron saint and was believed to appear on his white charger in their crucial battles to lead them to victory.

9 *Philip II*, by an artist of the school of El Greco. Fanatical in his religious convictions, the King was also a painstaking bureaucrat and an enlightened patron of the arts.

10 Lope de Vega was the most famous and prolific author of the Golden Age. In addition to poetry and novels, he wrote a vast number of plays, of which about 500 have survived.

11 *Philip IV*, by Velásquez, his court painter. Under Philip's reign, though great art and literature were still produced, Spain's political and economic decline set in.

12 *The Vision of Pedro de Salamanca* by Zurbarán. The Golden Age was also the age of St Iganatius Loyola, St Teresa, St John of the Cross, and many other saints and mystics.

13 *The Family of Charles IV* by Goya. After a phase of 'enlightened despotism', the Bourbon dynasty sank into dullness and degeneracy, as brilliantly suggested by Goya's brush.

14 The Inquisition was a ruthless machine for enforcing religious and political conformity. But it bred intolerance and fear, and ultimately sapped the nation's intellectual vitality.
15 *The Expulsion of the Moriscos* (1609). Though nominally christianized, the fear that the Moslems would act as a 'fifth column' led to their expulsion. 16 *The Second of May,* by Goya. Napoleon sent troops to occupy Spain but the people rose against them on 2 May 1808 and sparked off the Peninsular War.
17 *Guernica,* by Picasso. The bombing of the historic Basque town during the Civil War was a foretaste of the horrors which many European cities were soon to suffer.

18 Generalissimo Francisco Franco, victor in the Civil War and for three decades the master of Spain. 19 Don Juan Carlos, said to be favoured by Franco as heir to the throne. 20 Students demonstrating in Madrid, June 1968. Opposition to the Franco régime has been strong in the Spanish universities.

4 The aftermath of Empire

SEVEN CENTURIES OF RECONQUEST ascending to a brief peak of imperial greatness and then dropping away to a long decline – such is the graph of Spanish history. One can plot the descending curve in many different ways. There is a series of territorial losses, starting in 1640 with Portugal's successful (and Catalonia's unsuc׳ cessful) bid for independence, followed by the separation of the United Provinces, then that of the Catholic Low Countries, the cession of the Franche׳Comté and other provinces to France, the loss of the Italian possessions, Gibraltar, and for a time Minorca, and finally the emancipation of all Spanish America. There is the decadence of the Hapsburg dynasty – the insipid Philip III, the cultivated but profligate Philip IV, the pitiful Carlos II, 'the Bewitched', followed by a French dynasty whose rule was never fully in accord with the spirit of Spain. There is the dead hand of the Inquisition insulating the country from the current of European thought and stifling all signs of creative originality. There is the deepening mood of disillusionment, the loss of Spain's faith in her own mission – what Ganivet describes as *abulia* or paralysis of the national will; the recurrent financial crises and the economic stagna׳ tion; the exhaustion, through her wars and imperial exertions, of Spain's human resources, the depopulation of Castile, and the general demographic decline. There is the proliferation of paupers, pícaros, and priests. Exactly how these phenomena interact, which processes are cause and which effect, are questions which have aroused much debate. But the general pattern of the decline is undeniable, and some of its features are clear enough.

One is the bitter irony that the wealth of the Indies should have ended by impoverishing Spain. The influx of bullion set off a disastrous inflation and caused prices to rise four hundred per cent in the course of the sixteenth century. At first, the plunder of the Aztec and Inca empires brought fabulous bonanzas, and Spanish agriculture and industry were temporarily stimulated by the need to supply the growing colonies. Seville, thanks to its trade with the colonies, knew a dazzling prosperity. But production could not keep pace with demand. As prices rose, the plight of the poorer classes grew more desperate, and it was precisely those classes, particularly in Castile, which bore the mounting burden of taxation. A quarter of a million of the King's wealthiest subjects claimed noble rank, and thus exemption from taxation, and collected round them a thickening swarm of servants and hangers-on. The younger sons of hidalgo families, excluded from the succession by the handing down of entailed estates under the mayorazgo system, swelled the ranks of the 'unproductive classes' by seeking careers in the traditional fields of Church, army and royal service. The size of the mayorazgos increased through marriage and led to the concentration of more and more land in fewer hands. Moreover, the mayorazgo craze spread to ever wider sections of society and led to its increasing ossification at the very time when, in other parts of Europe, a spirit of capitalist enterprise was beginning to release the vigorous new forces which were to create the modern industrialized state.

Spain could not shake off her medieval outlook nor adjust her values to the needs of a changing society. During the Reconquest, rank and wealth had been won by force of arms; now the nation was everywhere on the defensive, and the French victory at Rocroi (1643) destroyed once and for all the myth that Spain's tercios were invincible. Commerce had been left mainly to Jews, manual labour to serfs and subject Moors; the expulsion of the Jews and finally of the Moriscos (1609) deprived Spain of some of her most useful citizens. The contrast between the nation's pretensions and the grim reality of her plight became so striking that it could no longer be ignored. All sorts of schemes, many of them hare-brained, were propounded for putting things right. One great minister, the Count of Olivares, threw himself into the task with commendable but often misguided energy, but the task was beyond him. The nation continued to decline and the Hapsburg dynasty sank to extinction. In 1700 a new dynasty – that of the Bourbons – was called in, and after a dozen years of warfare, in which Catalonia, with British and Austrian backing, supported a rival claimant, made good its hold on the throne and prepared to lead Spain to new destinies.

THE FRENCH CENTURY

The Bourbons, a French dynasty, set about applying French methods of centralism and absolutism to their new domains. The Catalans now paid the penalty for having backed the losing side in the wars of the succession. The Castilian court had swept away the whole structure of councils, regional Cortes, constitutional rights and fueros, against which Olivares had battled in vain. The Basque provinces and Navarre came off more lightly, for they had taken the side of Castile and the Bourbons. But Barcelona and Valencia were shorn of almost everything that had made up their distinctive identities. Almost—but not quite everything; for by pruning away their local peculiarities and forcing them into the common framework and wider markets of a unitary state, the Bourbons opened up to them the possibility of a vigorous new economic development. Gradually their agriculture began to revive, trade flourished, and their merchant fleet expanded. An important new textile industry was built up. The monopoly formerly enjoyed by Seville (and later Cadiz) was abolished, and trade with the American possessions was opened to all Spanish ports. Catalonia was not alone in benefiting from the resulting growth of prosperity, but economic revival was more marked and more rapid there than in other parts of the country. The economic centre of gravity thus began to shift away from the geographical, administrative and political core of the peninsula to its periphery. Castile succeeded in imposing the full weight of its hegemony on Catalonia just as the latter was beginning to surpass it in population, wealth and commercial vigour. The tensions set up by this dichotomy have shaped Spain's subsequent history, and lie at the heart of the 'Catalan question' today.

Thus the face of Spain began to change under the impact of the Bourbon reforms. Roads and canals were built. The dirty, higgledy-piggledy capital gradually took on the aspect of a well-designed eighteenth-century city. The forerunner of a national bank was established, manufacturing encouraged and some order brought into the nation's chaotic finances. An effort was made to clear the bandit-infested Sierra Morena and bring more land under cultivation by establishing settlements of German farmers. Radical plans were drawn up to counter the agricultural stagnation which had reduced the labouring population of Andalusia to the verge of starvation. The powerful Mesta organization, which for centuries had sub-ordinated settled agriculture to the interests of the owners of trans-humant sheep, was abolished. The Bourbons attempted to curb the mayorazgo system and the Church's appetite for land. Even the stultifying Inquisition was shorn of some of its powers, and in 1767 the Society of Jesus was expelled from the domains of the Spanish Crown.

The period of 'Enlightenment' reached its height under the reign of Charles III (1759–88). Powerful ministers like Aranda, Florida-blanca, Campomanes, Olavide and Jovellanos were men nurtured by the spirit of the Encyclopaedia and French rationalism, who sought to lift Spain out of her backwardness by the promotion of 'useful knowledge'. They believed that the welfare of the nation could best be served by increasing the power of the Crown and its centralized bureaucracy. Though groups of similarly 'enlightened' men banded together in different parts of Spain into 'Societies of Friends of the Country' to co-operate in the cause of reform, there was no question of encouraging the participation of wider sections of the population in public affairs through the old municipalities or cortes. The govern-ment of eighteenth-century Spain remained a despotism, though an enlightened one. It was an age which has left little great literature behind, for masterpieces are not written to order, and writers tended to lose touch with the springs of popular creativity. Good work was done by authors like Feijoo (1676–1764), who tilted tire-lessly against the ignorance and superstitions of the day, and the Jesuit satirist Isla, whose 'Father Gerundio' sought to debunk the pomposities of the pulpit, as Cervantes' Don Quixote had debunked the absurdities of the cult of knight errantry. Academies of History and Letters were founded in an attempt to raise the general cultural level of the nation. How badly this was needed we can tell from a work which, more than any other perhaps of the period, can still be read with pleasure – the *Life* of Torres Villaroel (1693–1770), whose adventures as student, soldier, hermit, fencing master, doctor, bull-fighter, maker of almanacs and professor of mathematics and astrology give us fascinating glimpses of a Spain still little touched by the spirit of Enlightenment.

It is in painting, not literature, that the Spain of the French century is most vividly reflected. 'This I saw', is the laconic comment which Goya affixed in place of a title to some of his most moving sketches. The canvases, drawings and etchings of that inexhaustible genius, many of them housed today in Madrid's Prado Museum, itself a fine example of late eighteenth-century design, present a panorama of the entire age. Here, in the series of cartoons commissioned for the royal tapestries we see the people of Spain in their fiestas and daily labours; high society, which Goya came to know through his duties as court painter, and whose reigning beauty, the Duchess of Alba, was for a time his mistress; Wellington, on his war horse; Godoy, the favourite, lolling with marshal's baton on a field of mock victory; the inane, complacent King Charles IV and his sensual, sly, prematurely aged Queen; the terrifying scenes of May 1808, when the populace rose against the French armies, the crimes and misery of the Disasters of War, leading to Goya's private world of macabre fantasy and near madness, the *Caprichos* and the 'black paintings'.

The attempts by the ministers of enlightened despotism to pro-mote prosperity by imposing reforms without allowing the people more political participation resemble in some respects those made by the 'technocrats' of Spain's present authoritarian régime in the direction of greater economic, but not political progress. The eighteenth-century experiment suffered from serious defects. One was its dan-gerous dependence on the personality of the king and the calibre of his all-powerful ministers. When Charles III was succeeded by the fatuous Charles IV, it became clear that the Bourbons, like the

Hapsburgs before them, were heading down the path of dynastic degeneracy. Affairs of state were left in the hands of the frivolous and scheming Queen María Luisa, and of her paramour and chief Minister, Godoy. The gulf between the people and this corrupt court widened ominously. They had rioted in protest against the attempts of one of Charles III's ministers to forbid the wearing of the traditional Spanish long cloak and wide-brimmed sombrero in favour of the short cloak and three-cornered hat of French fashion. In March 1808 the people rose to demand the resignation of Godoy, and soon afterwards the abdication of the king himself. Here was a new portent in Spanish history – the rising of the people in arms against an unworthy king. They were soon to vent their fury against a still more odious and alien authority.

The system of enlightened despotism was vulnerable from another quarter. It was all very well to promote 'useful knowledge'. But who could tell whether some ideas might prove not useful but dangerous? The men of Spain's Enlightenment watched with alarm as revolutions broke out beyond the frontiers. At the execution of the French king alarm deepened into horror and fear. The optimism and reforming zeal of the *esprits forts* hardened into reaction. The advent of Napoleon replaced the risk of revolutionary infection by other dangers. The Emperor needed Spain for his designs of European hegemony and for his wars against England. But he needed a reliable ally, not a country weakened by court intrigue and administrative chaos. Summoning both the dethroned Charles IV and his son Ferdinand VII to Bayonne, he forced an act of abdication from each of them and set up his own brother on the throne of Spain under the name of Joseph I. At the beginning of 1808 he poured more troops into the Peninsula both to consolidate the conquest of Portugal, which had previously been undertaken with the co-operation of the pliant Godoy, and to ensure the effective occupation of Spain itself.

On 2 May, 1808, the people of Madrid turned on the French with whatever weapons they could find. Marshal Murat, completely mis-judging the proud national temper, thought he could cow the Spaniards into submission by brutal reprisals. Soon all Spain was in arms. The bureaucracy built up under the Bourbons disintegrated;

patriotic *juntas* sprang up everywhere to lead the struggle and to form rudimentary local administrations. The junta of Seville raised a militia which inflicted a resounding defeat on the French at Bailén, forcing Joseph, the 'intruder king' to flee. Although he later returned to re-establish a precarious authority over some parts of Spain, the struggle which we know as the Peninsular War and the Spaniards call the War of Independence continued for six years and constituted the first sustained check to Napoleon's designs for continental domination. Apart from the operations of the small British expeditionary force under Moore and Wellington, the war was mainly an affair of fierce harassment by guerrilla bands. They avoided pitched battles – the most famous of the guerrilla leaders known as El Empecinado, the Indomitable, claimed that he had never lost a single man in a formal engagement – and weakened the enemy by tying down large numbers in unfriendly territory. The Spanish people astonished the world, as in General Palafox's desperate defence of Saragossa, by their heroism. But the anarchically independent juntas could only with difficulty be brought to co-operate together. When at length a central junta was established and a cortes convened at Cadiz, a liberal but quite unworkable Constitution was proclaimed (1812) and a Regency set up pending the return of Ferdinand VII.

The collapse of royal authority led to the appearance of local juntas in Spain's overseas domains as well. There the political implications were more serious, for the desire for independence, or at least for more self-government, had been steadily increasing amongst the Creoles, or American-born Spaniards. The reforming zeal of enlightened despotism had, paradoxically, only fanned the flames of their resentment. What the Creoles wanted was the chance to manage their own affairs and to trade as they wished. Their foiling of attempts by the British to establish themselves in Montevideo and Buenos Aires in 1806 made the Creoles aware of their new power and of the benefits they could expect from the abolition of Spain's old trading restrictions. The setting up of juntas professing loyalty to the captive Ferdinand VII led inevitably to the declaration of complete independence. An exhausted and divided Spain, obsessed with its own internal difficulties, was in no position to re-impose its rule. By the second quarter of the nineteenth century, Spain's vast American empire, with the exception of the Caribbean islands of Cuba and Puerto Rico, was no more.

In 1814, Ferdinand 'the Desired' returned to his country. Those who had expected from his restoration a new era of peace, national reconciliation and progress, were to be bitterly disillusioned. Though he had publicly pledged his readiness to lead the country along the constitutional path, he soon repudiated the 1812 Constitution and began a savage persecution of all those who had striven to lay the foundations for a Liberal Spain. His rule of repression and reaction was buttressed by the calling in of another French army, 'the hundred thousand sons of St Louis'. Thus, a century and a quarter after the advent of the Bourbon dynasty, absolutism once again reigned supreme in Spain with the help of French bayonets.

LIBERALS VERSUS TRADITIONALISTS

If there is any pattern to be discerned beneath the political chaos of the period between 1814 and 1931 it is that of the polarization into Liberals and Traditionalists, Radicals and Catholic Conservatives, and finally, in our own times, into revolutionaries and reactionaries. Even when that fatal process was yet in its early stages, the tragic and gifted Romantic poet Larra (1809–37) could compare his country to a graveyard: 'here lies half Spain, done to death by the other half'. The key-stone of old Spain had been the monarchy. The mob which rose in arms against the French still clamoured for the return of their King, Ferdinand 'the Desired'. Yet his widow was before long to be forced from the regency and his daughter, Queen Isabel, from the throne. The monarchy was briefly replaced by a republic (1873) and, after a restoration which showed that the Crown had become a factor for discord rather than national unity, discarded anew (1931).

With this key-stone knocked from the old edifice of state, few institutions were left capable of countering the centrifugal tendencies of Spanish life. One was the army. Hence a new feature of the political scene: the advent of the soldier-politician. The first dramatic intervention came from a group of officers awaiting embarkation for the South American wars who led their troops instead against Ferdinand's government and forced him for a time to respect the 1812 Constitution. This was the first of several cases of military intervention in the Liberal interest, for many disgruntled officers who had done well in the days of guerrilla warfare found that the Restoration had little use for their services. There was intervention, too, by Conservative supporters. This was to be expected, for the military mind saw the country's problems in terms of the maintenance of order and traditional values. The soldier-politician believed that he had a mission as guardian of the public weal against the shilly-shallying of civilian politicians. Military intervention became aptly known as a *pronunciamiento*; the officer had only to 'pronounce', not to debate, nor to attempt the difficult task, so uncongenial to the Spanish temperament, of seeking a consensus between contending opinions. The soldier-politician was, by definition, authoritarian. He also tended to be narrowly Catholic in the tradition of Santiago Matamoros, which identified political opponents as godless rebels to be destroyed. According to one story when the military dictator, Narváez, lay on his death-bed and was asked by his confessor whether he had forgiven all his enemies, the General replied with a good conscience: 'I have no enemies, Father; I have had them all shot'.[28]

The Church, although its influence was to revive later in the century, had declined both spiritually and materially. The men of the Enlightenment had looked with disfavour on the proliferation of 'useless monks', and the Liberals were to inherit their view. Priests and monks had been the life and soul of popular resistance to the French, who had desecrated churches and closed monasteries. The Liberals' legislation reduced the power and wealth of the Church still further; and from 1835 Church lands were secularized and sold together with many entailed estates and communal lands. A new class of *parvenu* landowner was thus brought into existence, bound to the Liberal interest through the acquisition of these properties. Though Spain was long to remain a fanatically religious country permitting only the exercise of the Catholic faith – as George Borrow was to discover in his endeavours to peddle the Bible – the Church underwent the same process of polarization which was reshaping the general life of the nation. Bitterly hostile to the Liberals for reasons of dogma and material interest, Catholicism came to be more and more identified with the conservative and upper classes. Sporadic church, burnings and the murder of priests showed that popular fanaticism was beginning to assume an anti-clerical hue. Only in certain rural areas of the north, particularly in the Basque provinces and Navarre, did the Church continue to command unquestioning loyalty. Here the phenomenon known as Carlism was to flourish, and still finds its sympathizers today.

The movement took its name from Don Carlos, the rigidly reactionary brother of Ferdinand VII, whose despotism had been tempered by the temporizing of the born trimmer. Don Carlos stood for a reversion to the old theocratic kingship of the sixteenth century; but he based his claim to the throne on the French Salic Law which barred women from the succession, and conveniently ignored Spain's own tradition which had made the reign of the first Queen Isabel possible. In the Carlist creed, the fanatically conserva, tive Catholicism of the Basque peasantry merged with their attach, ment to their ancient fueros to produce seven years of civil war (1833–40), to be followed by further outbreaks in the course of the century – that of 1873 giving them control of most of the north of Spain as far as the Ebro – under successive and sometimes rival pretenders. The Carlists were masters of guerrilla warfare, which readily degenerated into brigandage and pillage. Their movement was the protest of tradition-loving highlanders against the more liberal, minded cities.

The Liberals were themselves divided into moderates and *exal, tados* or progressives, and tended too often to look for support from the army rather than from a broad-based following in the country. Isabel had been forced to rely on the Liberals in her struggle against the Carlists, but her own bigotry, together with the scandals of her private life, at length led to her abdication (1868). A period of con, fusion and wild experimentation followed. A well-intentioned Italian prince, Amadeo, was offered the throne but soon stepped down from his uneasy seat. Next there occurred a brief republican interlude (1873), nurtured by the ideas of the French writer Proudhon and of a dedicated but impractical theoretician, Pi y Margall. He was one of the four presidents who succeeded each other at the head of the young republic within a year, when the pent-up forces of regionalism and local patriotism burst forth and quickly reduced the country to anarchy. The Liberals had believed no less fervently than the Bour-bons in the virtues of centralism, and had attempted to reduce the particularist spirit of the old historic divisions of Spain by subdividing the country into the forty-nine provinces which are still the basis for Spanish administration today. The Federalists reacted against this by encouraging the emergence of 'cantons' which they believed would govern themselves and co-operate spontaneously for the common good on a national scale. Particularly in Catalonia, the Levante and Andalusia, society dissolved into a chaos of competing towns and even villages, each proclaiming its own sovereignty and, in some cases as in Alcoy, the social revolution preached by the Anarchists. Matters were made worse by the threatened disintegration of the army, the defection of most of the navy to the 'Canton' of Cartagena, and a fresh Carlist rising in the north. Spain, true to its fateful propensity to go from one extreme to another, was rapidly swinging from centralism to complete fragmentation, from order to anarchy, when to the relief at least of the now thoroughly alarmed middle classes, another general emerged to reverse the process and summon Queen Isabel's son Alfonso from his school in England to the throne of his fathers.

The restoration of the monarchy did not, however, mean the triumph of reaction. Outwardly, Spain appeared to have chosen the path of parliamentary democracy, with a constitutional monarch, free elections and a two-party system. But elections were rigged and the party system manipulated to ensure the rotation in office of groups of politicians and their clients who could all count in time on getting a share of the spoils. This sham parliamentarianism was the work of Cánovas del Castillo, the dominating political figure of the day. At least it gave Spain some years of sorely needed peace and econo-mic development, thanks largely to the growing interest of foreign capital, which had already built most of the country's rail network and was now eager to exploit its rich resources of iron, copper and lead. Spain was astir too with new intellectual currents. The great educational reformer, Giner de los Ríos, was beginning to mould a new generation of liberal teachers, thinkers and scientists, through his Instituto Libre de Enseñanza, a formidable challenge to the Church's traditional monopoly of all education. The Church, for its part, was experiencing a certain spiritual renovation and regaining much of its hold over the upper and middle classes, so that each side was regrouping its forces for a fresh round in the struggle between Liberals and Clericals.

Nowhere is Restoration Spain, with its Madrid menabouttown, indolent civil servants and social climbers, its decayed aristocrats, earnest intellectuals and entrepreneurs, its robust women of the people, beggars and narrowminded provincial *beatas*, more vividly portrayed than in the novels of Pérez Galdós (1843–1920). He was a writer comparable to Balzac in his vast output and range of human understanding, and to Scott in his power of evoking, in the fortysix volumes of the *Episodios Nacionales*, the panorama of his country's past. Nevertheless, for all its vitality and growing prosperity, Restoration Spain was based on a system flawed by fatal political weaknesses. It led to increasing corruption and cynicism and confirmed the conviction of army officers that they would one day return to fulfil their destiny as 'saviours of their country'. The Cánovas system also denied the mass of the people any real say in the running of their country's affairs. Between them and the politicians in Madrid stood a vast host of fixers – the *jefes políticos* in the towns, and *caciques*, or local bosses, in the rural areas, who together saw to it by patronage or intimidation that the right candidates were returned at elections. Cánovas declared, somewhat too complacently, that though the surface might be troubled, the depths of Spain's national life remained limpid and serene. Dangerous currents, however, were stirring in the depths, and before the end of the century, Cánovas had been assassinated and the whole nation been shaken by a fresh disaster.

In 1898, the United States intervened in the struggle which Spain had been waging intermittently for more than three decades to reduce her rebellious Cuban subjects to obedience. The crushing defeats inflicted on her by the Yankees, and the loss of her last colonies brought home to the nation the humiliating extent of their backwardness and the ineptitude of their government and armed forces. A mood of bitter heart-searching set in. What was the cause of this decadence, what was Spain's new role in the modern world, the destiny of her people? The writers, teachers and journalists who began to concern themselves with these questions and to give their highly individual answers formed a brilliant galaxy. A few, like Azorín (1873–1967), the evocative essayist of provincial Castile, and the Galician poet and novelist Valle Inclán (1866–1936), were apolitical artists whose message was implicit in the quality of their work. Most of the group were journalists of genius, for the public could best be roused and instructed through the press. The Generation of Ninety-Eight is the term loosely applied to these writers, though one of the most gifted of their number, Angel Ganivet (1865–98), was driven by private grief, not political despair, to take his own life in that same year. The author of the *Idearium Español* had lost his faith but clung instead to the stoicism which he held to be an essential element in his country's genius, yet he recognized Catholicism as its central tradition, and also the formative importance of the Moslem, African impact. Other members of the Generation of Ninety-Eight were more thoroughgoing advocates of 'Europeanization'. Joaquín Costa (1844–1911), a forceful and erudite Aragonese, campaigned for 'School and Larder' – educational and agrarian reform – and demanded that the Traditionalists should 'lock, and lock again, the tomb of the Cid', so that Spain might rid herself of harmfully anachronistic ideals. Ortega y Gasset (1883–1955), the most influential publicist of all, was an admirer of German culture and science. In his *Revolt of the Masses* (1930) he warned against the rising tide of mediocrity threatening to engulf the élite which he believed to be the necessary leaven for any healthy society and in his *Invertebrate Spain* (1921) he offered an illuminating analysis of the centrifugal and centripetal forces at play within his own country. Another interesting figure was Ramiro de Maeztu (1874–1936), son of a Basque father and an English mother. After spending a number of years as a press correspondent in England, Maeztu evolved into a champion of

Catholic traditionalism and of the creed of *Hispanidad* which the Falange was later to take up. Perhaps the greatest of all the Generation of Ninety-Eight was another Basque, Miguel de Unamuno (1864–1936). The Basque, it has been said, is the quintessential Spaniard, for in him the Spaniard's individualism finds its most obsessive and forceful expression. This is certainly true of Unamuno, in whose own overpowering and combative personality the opposite extremes of the Spanish temperament – the Catholic traditionalist and the radical Europeanizer – seemed to co-exist and clash. His books are battlefields, in which the unending struggle between faith and reason is fought out with fierce intensity. Unamuno's theme is Man – not man in the abstract, but the man of flesh and blood, involved in the problem of the society around him, and above all, involved in the cosmic problem of human destiny. Unamuno is thus the most Spanish and at the same time the most universal of writers; Spanish, in such books as his fascinating exploration of the national character and destiny, *The Life of Don Quixote and Sancho*, universal in his existentialist meditations on the human condition, his great philosophical work, *The Tragic Sense of Life*.

While intellectuals were engaged in this process of national stock-taking, new creeds were competing for the allegiance of Spain's growing working-class. Marxian Socialism appealed to the authoritarian and institutional bent of the Castilians; Anarchism to the libertarian spirit of the Catalan workers, whose radicalism was intensified by an influx of rootless, illiterate labourers from Murcia and Andalusia. The proletariat, no less than other sections of the nation, was thus subject to its own process of polarization which was in time to bring fatal consequences. The Socialist-controlled General Workers Union (UGT) fought for their rights within the existing social order; the Anarchists were predominant in the National Confederation of Labour (CNT), refused to have any truck with the bourgeoisie, and abandoned themselves to messianic dreams of the new society which could only arise from a revolutionary cataclysm. The violent landmarks in their struggle were Barcelona's 'Tragic Week' of 1909, which started as a protest against attempts to call up conscripts for a campaign in Morocco and ended in the burning of churches and in large-scale street-fighting, and the wave of strikes which started in 1917 and were harshly suppressed by the Army. The Anarchists turned their bombs and their pistols not only against national political figures like Cánovas, but also against the wealthy bourgeoisie of Barcelona. During the Conservative premiership of Maura, the Conservative leader who tried to make Cánovas' sham parliamentarianism work, the Madrid politicians cynically connived at the Anarchist onslaught against the social sector which was also the backbone of Catalan nationalism. The latter movement had been stimulated by a linguistic and literary renaissance in the previous century and by the vigorous development of Catalan industry and commerce. So long as the country as a whole continued to profit from the demand for Spanish products created by the First World War (in which the country remained neutral) these social and national tensions could be held in check. But once Spain began to feel the pinch of the slump which followed the wartime boom, the system began to crack. 'Let those who make government impossible govern', exclaimed the weary Premier in 1922. The King, Alfonso XIII, had increasingly sought to make parliamentary government unwork-able by misusing his constitutional powers. Now he could turn to the military who had long been awaiting their cue in the wings.

The new dictator was General Primo de Rivera. Although his rule coincided with Mussolini's rise to power, and in spite of half-hearted attempts to ape Italian corporatism and form a political party of his own, Primo de Rivera was no Fascist. He was an Anda-lusian – shrewd, intuitive, garrulous and *simpático*, eager to enjoy the good things of life and to give them to his people, provided they knew their place under his paternalistic rule. Uninterested in ideas and contemptuous of the intellectuals and politicians, the dictator pro-claimed the simple verities of Country, Church and King, identi-fying himself with the first, leaving to the second its education and moral guidance, and little more than the trappings of royalty to the third. He came to terms with the Socialist-controlled trade unions, giving them the benefits of better housing and social services as the price of their obedience. The Anarcho-Syndicalists he suppressed with an iron hand, thereby compensating the Catalan bourgeoisie for the scant respect paid to their aspirations for greater autonomy. Primo de Rivera gave his country some impressive public works. In putting an end to Abd el Krim's rebellion and making a generous settlement with Morocco, he achieved at least one stroke of genuine statesmanship. But he made no serious attempt to solve the deep-rooted problems of a country that was growing ever more deeply divided. For seven years the dictator simply kept his finger tightly on the cork whilst the deadly brew continued to ferment. When the world economic crisis became serious, his one-time popularity declined and he realized too late that even the Army, on which his power depended, had been alienated by his high-handed rule. Primo de Rivera left for voluntary exile in France, where he died a few months later. The king, eager to requite himself for the slights received at the hands of the dictator, was not sorry to see him go, and desperately sought a successor who could tackle the difficult task of liberalizing what remained of his system. It was too late. The Crown had been irreparably discredited by its association with the dictatorship. The country had had enough of order and was crying out for liberty. Voices were raised, particularly in the cities, clamouring for a republic. In April 1931, King Alfonso XIII quietly followed Primo de Rivera into exile and Spain embarked on a new and fateful chapter of her history.

REPUBLIC AND CIVIL WAR

The Second Republic was ushered in with far higher hopes and more popular enthusiasm than had greeted the appearance of that experiment of idealistic intellectuals, the short-lived First Republic. About half the population, particularly in the towns, favoured a republic; the other half, mainly in the more conservative countryside, remained monarchist, even if they were not prepared to make a stand for an unpopular king. Could the moderate republicans win over and sustain a consensus of national opinion which would allow the country to find orderly and generally acceptable solutions to its basic problems? Would the Centre find itself fatally eroded by the extremists of the right and of the left? On the answer to this fateful question hung the whole future of republican Spain.

The first swing of the pendulum was predictable. Primo de Rivera had stood for clericalism, army supremacy and centralism; it was natural that the Republic should show itself anti-clerical, anti-military and in favour of regional autonomy. At first, it looked as if the great problems which the dictator had suppressed might be solved by reason and mutual consent. The Catalans, after teetering on the brink of complete separation, were induced to settle for full autonomy, as were the Basques. Unamuno returned to Salamanca amidst the plaudits of his students, and the government set about making up for years of educational neglect by a hurried programme of school build-ing. A new period of cultural freedom and creativity seemed possible. Labour was offered a more solid fare of social legislation through the pressure of Socialists anxious not to be outbid by their radical rivals, the Anarcho-Syndicalists. The peasants, too, looked to the 1932 Agrarian Law to alleviate their misery by breaking up the larger unworked estates in central and southern Spain. But the gov-ernment's reforming zeal cost the republic the enmity of the country's two most powerful institutions. The privileges of the Army, which had made it a state within a state by exempting it from the jurisdic-tion of the civilian courts and the criticism of the press, were abolished and the Captains General shorn of their power. The Church was disestablished, its funds cut down, its control of education, marriage and divorce brought to an end and its orders suppressed.

The Republic's life-span of five years falls into three periods; that of the moderate left (April 1931–mid 1933), the *Bienio Negro* or 'two black years' of right-wing republicanism (November 1933–February 1936), and the extremist Popular Front phase culminating in the outbreak of the Civil War in July 1936.

The leading figure of the first, hopeful, period was the Prime Minister Azaña, a civil servant of intellectual distinction and pro-bity, but aloof and touchy. His government had to face challenges from both the right and the left – an attempted *putsch* by General Sanjurjo in Seville and a wave of strikes. More serious were the dis-orders stemming from attempts to implement the agrarian reform, or from the authorities' failure to do so. Spain was still suffering from the effects of the world depression; low agricultural prices, which put land out of cultivation and labourers out of work. The govern-ment was handicapped by shortage of funds and trained personnel. Nor did they have any clear policy of what to put in place of the expropriated estates; should it be small peasant holdings or some form of collective co-operative ownership better suited perhaps to the needs of efficient dry farming? The tragic events at the village of Casas Viejas, where anarchist-led peasants attempted to take matters into their own hands and were exterminated by the Civil Guard, indicated the way the Republic might go.

The 1933 elections, at which some six million women voted for the first time, brought a swing to the right and a new government under the opportunist politician and ex-revolutionary demagogue Lerroux. More conservative Catholic opinion, alienated by the government's anti-clerical policies, rallied to a new grouping under the adroit leadership of Gil Robles. Still further to the right, and openly hostile to the Republic, were militant groups like the Falange, founded by José Antonio, son of the former dictator Primo de Rivera, which fused with another pro-Nazi group known as the Juntas de Ofensiva Nacional-Sindicalista (JONS). The growing militancy of the right provoked in turn a polarization to the left. Largo Caballero, the powerful trade union leader, ominously declaring that the Republic was being betrayed, sought to outstrip the Anarcho-Syndicalists and the Communists. The Anarchists made their bid with a rising in Saragossa, followed by the great strike of March 1934. The following October, when an attempt was made to strengthen the Lerroux cabinet by the inclusion of members from Gil Robles' party, came the turn of the Socialists. Their rebellion was quickly stamped out in Madrid and Barcelona, but the defiant miners of Asturias could only be quelled by the army. The officer entrusted with their suppression was the youngest general in the armed forces, an officer noted for his ruthless efficiency and reputed loyalty to the Republic: Francisco Franco.

The October rebellion left the Lerroux administration weakened and discredited, and the country one step nearer to civil war. The President of the Republic, Alcalá Zamora, had the choice of inviting Gil Robles, as leader of the largest party in the Cortes, to form an alternative government, or of calling for new elections. Distrusting the republican loyalties of the Conservatives, he took the latter course. The left formed an electoral alliance which returned them to power, but the extent of their triumph was deceptive. Though they were now a majority in the Cortes, the balance of forces in the country at large remained fairly evenly divided between right and left. Nor did the Popular Front government have the strength to rule effectively. The Anarchists refused to exercise power jointly with bourgeois politicians, and the Socialists were split between the partisans of Prieto, chief architect of the Popular Front, and the more uncompromising Largo Caballero. As for the right, the moderate conservative following of Gil Robles gravitated towards the Falange, or the militant nationalism proclaimed by Calvo Sotelo, Primo de Rivera's finance minister who had now returned from exile. The centre was fading from Spain's political spectrum, leaving the irreconcilable extremes. Compromise, consensus, consent – words which never came easily to Spanish lips – vanished altogether from the vocabulary. The oratory of the council chamber was drowned by the clamour of the street. Each party had its squads of thugs and its semi-militarized youth formations who hunted down political opponents and clashed openly with their rival organizations. Churches were desecrated and monasteries burned down. Estates untouched by the lagging agrarian reform were invaded by revolutionary squatters and factories paralyzed by incessant strikes. In Navarre, Carlist *requetés* smuggled in arms and trained openly for the rising which should restore an authoritarian, Catholic, traditionalist monarchy. In the universities, Falangists battled with Marxists, whilst the disaffected officers of the Unión Militar Española conspired with right-wing groups, and the generals silently laid their plans.

The most forceful figure on the right was now Calvo Sotelo. He was shot down and his assassination sparked off the Civil War. This crime seems to have been no part of some communist plot, as was later claimed, but rather a reprisal by a group of Assault Guards for the murder of one of their comrades by the Falange. The next stage in the fatal escalation was a pronunciamiento by the generals on 17 July. The leading figures in the conspiracy were Sanjurjo, exiled in Lisbon after his abortive 1932 coup, Mola at Burgos, Queipo de Llano in the south, and Franco, who flew from his post in the Canary Islands in a chartered British plane to take command in Morocco. The latter, as had happened more than once in Spain's long history, had become the launching-pad for another invasion which was to change the face of the peninsula. But now, by an ironic twist of fate, the Moors were to fight under a Christian general who proclaimed a crusade against godless 'anti-Spain'.

The Civil War was the outcome of miscalculations on both sides. The generals claimed, as other officers had claimed during the previous one hundred years, that they were acting in the patriotic conviction that their country needed to be saved from misrule by incompetent and treacherous politicians, and that they had only to 'pronounce' for power to fall automatically into their hands. Their mistake was to assume that politics were still the preserve of the politicians and to ignore the growing determination of the people to shape their own affairs. The politicians, for their part, were unaccountably blind to the dangers of a military coup, and when it came, they held back for fear of unleashing the forces of social revolution. When they did decide to throw open the arsenals and arm the workers' militia it was in time to prevent the coup from becoming a take-over, but too late to stop it growing into a civil war.

In Morocco, where the army's influence was strong and its resentment against the Madrid politicians particularly fierce, the rebels quickly gained the upper hand. The crack troops of the Foreign Legion and the seasoned Moroccan troops led by Spanish officers gave their fanatical devotion to Franco as an officer whom they knew and trusted for his fearless and resolute leadership. In Seville, Queipo de Llano had seized control, though the Republic still commanded the loyalty of the Andalusian peasant masses. In Burgos, Mola was well placed to rally right-wing sympathies in Old Castile and the fanatical Carlist *requetés* of Navarre. But the industrial towns of the north remained republican strongholds, as did the great cities of Barcelona and Madrid, where the hastily armed workers' militias, stiffened by a few units of police, Civil Guards and the armed forces which remained loyal, savagely annihilated the garrisons

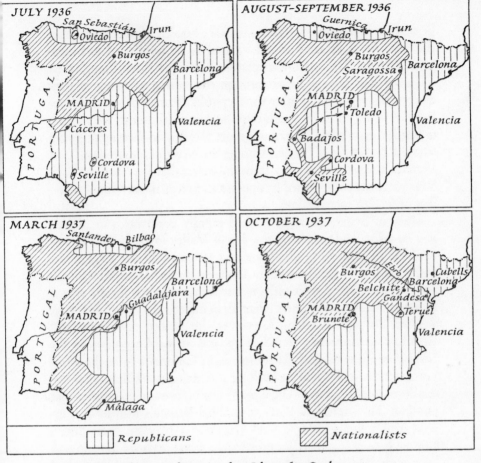

The Civil War: The course of operations from July 1936 to October 1937

attempting to seize control. In about two-thirds of the country, including the Levante and Catalonia, with its industrial potential, the initial rising failed. Sanjurjo died in an aeroplane crash whilst on his way from Lisbon to take over his command; Queipo de Llano and Mola were also to lose their lives in accidents in the course of the war, leaving Franco as the Generalissimo and supreme political leader of the rebellion.

As soon as it became clear that the pronunciamiento would not result in an immediate take-over, the rebels – or Nationalists as they

113

began to style themselves – aimed to strike a quick blow at the capital. But first, Franco's army in Africa had to be transferred to metropolitan Spain. The Straits were patrolled by ships which, though their efficiency had been reduced through the killing of many of their officers, still remained loyal to the Republic. Franco solved the problem first by an airlift in which some 15,000 of his troops were flown to Seville, mainly in German transport planes, and then by shipping over the remainder of his forces under the escort of Italian naval and aircraft. It thus became clear from the outset that the Spanish Civil War was to be complicated by another and more sinister dimension – that of foreign intervention.

Once in Spain, the army pushed rapidly northwards to Mérida and Badajoz, and thence up the Tagus Valley towards Toledo and Madrid. In armament, discipline and tactical skill the Legionaries and Moors were clearly superior to the untrained levies who fought heroically to defend their villages but were no match for the enemy in open country. Prisoners were slaughtered, the wounded were finished off with the long knives of the Moors, and prominent Republican supporters rounded up and shot. According to the admission of the Nationalist commander, Colonel Yagüe, the number of victims herded into the bullring at Badajoz and killed amounted to almost two thousand. There may have been more than twice that number. The capture of Badajoz enabled Franco's men to link up with Mola's forces holding Old Castile and Navarre. Here things had not been going so well for the rebels. Their drive on Madrid had been hampered by lack of ammunition, and the Republicans had held them in the mountain passes north of the capital. With reinforcements from Franco, Mola was now able to clear the north-east, where the French frontier authorities were favouring the Republicans, much as the Portuguese were favouring the Nationalists in the west. Irún fell, Santander surrendered, and all but the extreme eastern end of the French frontier passed under the Nationalists' control.

In the meantime, the Nationalists had met with an unexpected check in their drive towards Madrid. Toledo remained in the hands of the Republicans, but the Nationalists had barricaded themselves in the massive Alcázar towering over the old city. The Republicans lacked the heavy artillery to reduce it, though with more time the Asturian miners would have undermined and blown up its massive fortifications. The resistance offered by the famished defenders became legendary. Today, the Alcázar has been rebuilt and preserved as a shrine to the 'Crusade'; amongst the exhibits is the battered telephone through which Colonel Moscardó, the commander of the fortress, spoke to his son whom the Republicans were holding hostage as a means of forcing the father to capitulate, and exhorted him to commend his soul to God and prepare to face the Reds' firing squad. The Alcázar was at last relieved, but only at the cost of diverting forces needed for crucial operations against Madrid. This respite gave the Republicans time to strengthen their positions and stiffen them with fighters of the International Brigades which had just reached the capital. Foreign intervention, this time from supporters of the left, was to help win this round for the Republic.

Both sides now set about organizing their respective territories for a long war. The Nationalists controlled the main food-producing areas but were faced with an acute labour shortage through the flight of large numbers of workers and peasants to the Republican lines and the imprisonment or execution of many of their leaders. A stern military government, sanctioned with the blessing of the Church, was set up. The seat of government was established at Burgos and later expanded to include civilians. Its first legislation (April 1938), repealing the Republic's laws on divorce, Catalan autonomy, and agrarian reform, left no doubt as to the authoritarian, reactionary character of the régime which the Nationalists intended to impose. In the Republican zone, a very different and frankly revolutionary mood prevailed. With Azaña as President, Largo Caballero headed a cabinet of Republicans, Socialists, Communists and (later) Anarchists, but real power lay with the labour organizations, each with its own armed militia, whose rivalries hindered the effective prosecution of the war. Both sides found themselves in control of populations which included a large number of suspected or declared enemies. Hence the use of terror, both by Republicans and Nationalists; the execution of hostages and prisoners (José Antonio, founder of the Falange, perished in this way) and the dread *paseos* – secret raids by armed gangs who would break into the homes of their victims and carry them off to execution. In the Nationalist zone, the terror was coldly calculated; in the Republican, especially in the Anarchist strongholds of Catalonia where cases of church-burning and the murder of priests were frequent, it tended to be more spontaneous and uncontrolled, and was often directed by one nominally allied faction against another. Yet despite these excesses, there prevailed amongst the Republicans a mood of idealist and naive enthusiasm which rapidly began to transform the whole economic and social structure. George Orwell, who was in Barcelona at the time, noted that 'practically every building of any size had been seized by the workers and was draped with red flags or with the red and black flag of the Anarchists; every wall was scrawled with the hammer and sickle and with the initials of the revolutionary parties; almost every church had been gutted and its images burnt . . . Every shop and café had an inscription saying it had been collectivized; even the bootblacks had their boxes painted red and black'.[29]

As the war went on, its grim lessons were carefully studied by the experts for the effects they might have on the course of the cataclysm which was soon to engulf all Europe. German, Italian and Russian advisers assessed the performance of their respective aircraft, armour and anti-tank weapons and put new tactics to the test. The Germans used Spain's ordeal as an opportunity for training the Luftwaffe, and the systematic bombing by the Condor Legion of the Basques, historical capital at Guernica set a precedent for the destruction of Warsaw, Rotterdam, Coventry and other cities in the Second World War.[30] The Germans and the Russians preferred to confine their intervention to the supply of arms, staff officers, technicians and small numbers of pilots and other highly trained personnel. They extracted a heavy price from their respective beneficiaries; Hitler secured favourable terms for the acquisition of valuable minerals such as tungsten which he required for his war industries, whilst Stalin insisted on being paid out of the gold reserves which the Republican Government transferred from the Bank of Spain to the Russian vaults where what remains of them lie hidden to this day. Mussolini favoured more spectacular intervention; he welcomed the war as a means of weakening the position of France and Britain in the Mediterranean, and hoped to gain the Balearics as a reward for openly committing large numbers of Italian troops. The latter strove to make a spectacular break-through of the Madrid defences, but their initial success was turned to a humiliating rout at the battle of Guadalajara (March 1937). Britain and France, alarmed at the prospect of a Spain under the influence of the hostile totalitarian states, tried unsuccessfully to get all the great powers to adhere to a policy of non-intervention. France, then under a Popular Front government, sympathized with the Republicans, but held back from helping them for fear of alienating Britain, whose support she deemed essential to her security in face of a resurgent Germany. The British Government, bent on a course of appeasement which was to culminate in the Munich Agreement, was in no mood to force the Axis powers to keep their hands off Spain. The international conjuncture thus told against the Republic and favoured the Nationalist cause.

The course of the war can be briefly told. On the Madrid front, a bitter stalemate of trench warfare, despite a major effort by the Republicans to break out to the south in the costly battle of Brunete (July 1937). Two other major Republican offensives; at Teruel, on the Aragonese front, where they cut off a Nationalist salient but could not hold it (winter of 1937/38), and south of the Ebro River, where they dented, but failed to pierce, the enemy lines (July–November 1938). Slowly the Nationalists' superiority in discipline, generalship and armaments gained the upper hand. In the south-east, Málaga was captured, with the merciless slaughter of civilians and fugitives (February 1937); the 'iron ring' round Bilbao was broken and Basque resistance crushed (June 1937); the Nationalists reached the Mediterranean coast, splitting the Republican armies in Catalonia and the Levante (April 1938); Barcelona was entered (January 1939) and finally, after a brief civil war within the besieged capital, where the Communists were foiled in their attempts to make a last-ditch stand, Madrid capitulated and the war was over (March–April 1939).

The victorious generalissimo had insisted on unconditional surrender. He had proved a wily and tenacious war leader, but it was not in his nature to show magnanimity in victory. In the aftermath of the Civil War, Larra's epitaph of a century before sounded more grimly appropriate than ever: 'Here lies half Spain, done to death by the hand of the other half'. A quarter of a million Republican refugees fled over the French border to seek asylum. The number of those who had perished on the battlefield, before the firing squad, or in other ways as a consequence of the war was officially put at one million and may not have been far less than that figure. The country was left with her communications disrupted, much of her industry destroyed and her agriculture neglected, many of her towns and villages in ruins, and what remained of her decimated labour force sullen and exhausted. Europe, soon to be engulfed in her own war, had little interest and few resources for the reconstruction of the ravaged peninsula. Spain was left to rebuild her future as best she could and as her new master decreed.

Nearly three decades have now passed and Spain has risen from the ashes. Devastation has given way to a new economic prosperity and a generation has arisen with little or no direct experience of the tragic 'thirties. Yet the trauma of that ordeal has not yet been wholly lifted and the Spain of today is still fashioned and ruled according to the will of the man who made and won the Civil War.

5   Franco's Spain—the political and economic scene

THE FRANCO REGIME is commonly referred to outside Spain as
a 'dictatorship', and the epithet 'Fascist' often thrown in for good
measure. The description is so loose as to be misleading, for in its
current political structure, as in much else, 'Spain is different'.
Though styling itself an 'organic representative democracy', it
certainly lacks the free institutions, political parties and channels for
free association and expression which we associate in the West with
democracy. The government is authoritarian and autocratic, but it is
not totalitarian. Franco does not rule through a monolithic power
machine but through the skilful balancing of forces, only one of
which, the now divided and discredited Falange, has some faded
Fascist colouring. Yet undeniably, in a Europe of integrating democratic states, a régime brought to power with the help of Hitler's
Luftwaffe and Mussolini's 'volunteers' seems offensively anachronistic. That the rest of Europe might think it so probably weighs little
with Franco.

Inside Spain itself, however, a new generation is arising who regard
the Civil War as past history and look to Europe for their future.
Can the authoritarian régime liberalize and adjust itself sufficiently
to win acceptance in a Europe which has cold-shouldered it politically for so long? Does Franco really *want* this liberalization, or is he
merely making empty gestures in this sense? What, in any case, will
follow when he goes? Are there new economic and social forces at
work which will make liberalization in the long run inevitable?

Constitutionally, Spain is a monarchy at present without a monarch. Its structure is defined by the *Fuero de los Españoles* of 1945 and

'legitimized' by the 1947 referendum approving the abolition of the republican form of government and the designation of Franco as the country's ruler for life, and by the 1966 referendum endorsing the new Organic Law which lays down guide-lines for the nation's future. The régime claims to be based on the three main 'organic' elements of society – the family, the municipality and the corporate labour-employer syndicates. Elections take place every three years, but are indirectly controlled by the government. The parliament, or Cortes, consists of up to 600 deputies (no longer known as *diputados*, as under the discredited Second Republic, but as *procuradores*, like those delegates whose power was broken by Charles V). One-third of them represent the *sindicatos*, one-fifth consist of elected 'heads of family', and the remainder represent the municipalities and provinces, the armed forces, the Church, cultural and profes-sional bodies and individuals selected directly by Franco himself. General Franco also nominates the president of the Cortes (who convokes and adjourns it at will and sets its agenda), appoints and dismisses all cabinet ministers and provincial governors, all heads of sindicatos, all armed forces commanders, even (by virtue of the 1953 Concordat) all bishops. Spain is thus ruled by the Caudillo with an absolutism equal to that of her Bourbon kings and with a tight personal control comparable to that exercised by Philip II. Franco indeed resembles that monarch – and perhaps models him-self consciously on him – in his patience and impassive self-control, in the simplicity of his domestic life coupled with an insistence on the ceremonial respect deemed his due, in his religiosity and sense of high vocation for the destiny of the nation as *Caudillo de España por la Gracia de Dios*. Like the Rey Prudente, Franco is noted for keeping his own counsel, his caution, his astuteness. Whereas Philip's pro-crastination undermined the vigour of an empire faced with the need for prompt and decisive action, Franco's bent for temporizing and masterly inactivity has given his exhausted country time to recover from civil war and has helped to establish his impregnable position. Franco claims that his mission is one of national reconcilia-tion. This he has sought to achieve not by any magnanimous gestures to the vanquished, but by stubbornly waiting for them to come to heel. In the hills not far away from the Escurial, he too has built his own monument – a gigantic cross towering over a monastery and an immense pantheon hewn out of the solid rock. Here, in the Valley of the Fallen, his bones will no doubt one day be laid beside those of the thousands who perished in the Civil War. But even in death the fallen may rest there only on the victor's terms. The pantheon contains at present only one name – the one to be found on the walls of every church in Spain – that of José Antonio Primo de Rivera, founder of the Falange and supreme martyr-symbol of the triumphant Crusade.

The Falange, or Phalanx, still bears the marks of its hybrid origins. Though himself the son of Primo de Rivera and an Andalusian *señorito*, whose background inspired confidence in ultra-conservative landowning and clerical circles, José Antonio also numbered radicals and anti-clericals amongst his followers. Besides being violently anti-democratic, he also bore a grudge against the monarchy for its supposed ill-treatment of his father, and anti-monarchal feeling is still a characteristic of the Falange today. After José Antonio's death, Franco forestalled a bid by the radical Falangist boss Hedilla to step into his shoes and himself took charge of the movement, which he then diluted with a motley assortment of army officers, conservatives and Carlists. After Franco's triumph, which coincided with the rising tide of Fascist and Nazi strength in Europe, Falangist ranks were swollen still further not only by opportunists and careerists, but by many socialists, anarchists and even communists seeking refuge from the victimization they would otherwise have to fear. Composed of such disparate elements and at length warned by the fate of Hitler's and Mussolini's movements, the Falange never imposed a full-blown ideology on the nation; still less did Franco allow it to dictate policy. It became instead a privileged 'establishment', licensed to dispense valuable patronage in government and official labour organizations. Sometimes – as when the monarchists conspired to take over the government in 1945 – Franco would unleash the Falange against monarchist, liberal or socialist opponents. When he judged the internal or external situation opportune, he would withdraw his favour and reshuffle his cabinet. In theory, since no political parties were permitted, all sound elements in the nation, whether members of the Falange or not, formed a consensus referred to as the National Movement. In practice, the non-Falangist sectors have played no more than a token part in this amorphous grouping, though Franco likes to keep open the option of setting up one group and putting down another within the framework of his all-embracing 'Movement'.

Even though he reshuffles the cards within the National Movement pack, Franco keeps one unchallengeable trump: the Army. It is the Army which has moulded his character and thinking, carried him to power, which it now shares with him and continues to guarantee. Together with the efficient police forces, which are also under military control, the Army remains the ultimate sanction of his régime. Its loyalty to the Caudillo is absolute. The officers who served under him in the Civil War hold posts of the greatest power and prestige in the nation. It is to the Army that Franco turns to suppress any challenge to his authority, as in the disbanding of the Falange's armed militia in 1944 and the curbing of bloodshed between students and Falangist squads in 1956. Such intervention has increased the Army's popularity amongst the many Spaniards who have little love for the Falange. Less applauded has been the activity of its military tribunals in sentencing, imprisoning, or executing Franco's political prisoners, such as the clandestine communist agent Julián Grimau captured in 1963. Now the generals who fought under Franco in the Civil War – though the Army is still over-weighted with them – are growing old, and before long must disappear. The Army is changing its structure and possibly – though no one can say for sure – its outlook. The once preponderant influence of Germany has been succeeded, since the 1953 defence agreements, by that of the United States. With the acceptance of sophisticated new equipment and training methods, a new spirit of professionalism has begun to develop. The younger officers no longer come forward in such numbers from those middle- and upper-class homes who traditionally look to the Army for a career and hold rigid conservative and Catholic views. A recent study has shown that a high proportion of cadets in the military academies are now the sons of NCO's or of officers who have risen from the ranks.[31] This does not cast doubt on their loyalty to the present régime, but it does suggest the likelihood of more radical 'Young Turk' or 'Nasserite' sympathies developing amongst the officer corps with regard to the sort of régime they would like to see succeeding that of Franco.

Amongst the older officers, as indeed with many in the Spanish middle and upper classes, the monarchy still commands considerable sympathy. Few believe that there is likely to be any restoration so long as Franco lives. Most monarchists content themselves with the vague prospects held out by the 1947 Succession Law and the Organic Law of 1966 which stipulate that Franco's successor (who may be a Regent, not King) must be loyal to the principles of the National Movement and relegate his choice to the cabinet and a council of notables called the Consejo del Reino. First in the line of succession – since his two elder brothers have formally renounced their right to it – is Don Juan, third son of the late King Alfonso XIII. Born in 1913, Don Juan was trained as a naval officer, served for a time with the British Navy, and is now regarded as a man of democratic and pro-Western outlook. Though he has at times openly criticized the Franco régime, he maintains correct if not cordial relations with the Caudillo, and occasionally returns to Spain for short visits from his self-imposed exile in Portugal. By agreement with Franco, his son Juan Carlos has been educated in Spain and it is generally thought that the greater pliancy of the young prince would make Franco regard him as a more acceptable successor. Don Juan, however, has let it be known that he has no intention of renouncing his rights in favour of his son. Nor are Don Juan and Don Juan Carlos the only pretenders. The Carlists favour Don Javier or his son Don Hugo Carlos de Bourbon Parma who has some considerable following in Navarre. Another possible claimant is an able young banker, Don Alfonso, son, through a morganatic marriage, of ex-King Alfonso's eldest son, Don Jaime. With so many claimants, the question of the succession has deliberately been left vague. Nor is it possible to say how much support there would be throughout the country for a restoration of the monarchy. If the prospect commands the enthusiasm of a few and the acceptance of most of the upper and middle classes, it might well meet with indifference and scepticism, if not hostility, from working people.

If we look behind the military and institutional power structure to assess the political support on which Franco's régime rests, we shall thus see that it is far from monolithic. At one end of the spectrum there is the Falange; next, in a position of expectant semi-legality, come the Monarchists; then other Catholic groups, ranging from the Conservatives to the Liberal and Radical wings. Imperceptibly and fluctuating, support shades off into opposition, until we pass to the specifically clandestine left-wing groups, the Socialists and the Communists. The Catholic middle sections of the spectrum may be more readily observed. The conservative Christian Democrats have at times served in Franco's cabinet as more palatable alternatives to the Falangists in a Europe where Christian Democrat governments have held power; but their best known leader, the veteran politician Gil Robles – also a stout Monarchist – must now be ranked with the opposition, though he has not seen the inside of Franco's jails. Some of the ablest of Franco's ministers are associated with the Catholic movement known as Opus Dei, which we shall be looking at more closely. Further on the Catholic left is the radical Christian Democrat group led by Jiménez Fernández, author of the Second Republic's agrarian reform law which sought to break the power of Spain's landed interests. Some sections of Catholic opinion bear no political label but veer from qualified support of the régime to qualified disapproval, generally in the wake of some commanding figure. One example of the latter type is Franco's former Minister of Education and Minister to the Vatican, Ruiz Giménez, a liberal Catholic who attended the Second Vatican Council and later openly criticized Franco's régime for its repressive nature. Another is Dionisio Ridruejo, formerly the Falange's most fanatical supporter and propagandist and now its bitterest foe.

Though smashed by defeat in the Civil War and by the hounding of Franco's police, there are still Socialists and Communists in Spain – how many, and how strong, it is impossible to say. The Socialists, as once the leading elements in the Republic, have been the special target of persecution. Attempts by their exiled leaders to rebuild an underground party in Spain have been repeatedly penetrated by the government's agents and the clandestine organizers hunted down. The Socialists are still believed to command sympathy amongst the workers and in the universities though it can find little overt expression. The same sections of the population have been the object of particular attention on the part of the Communists, who are probably better organized than the Socialists. The Communists also have the advantage of a powerful broadcasting station, 'Radio España Independiente' which is believed to operate from somewhere in Eastern Europe. In the early years of the Franco régime, the Communists formed armed bands on the French side of the Pyrenees which attempted to reenter Spain. These attempts failed and the Communists have long abandoned armed action in favour of non-violent 'united front' tactics with the object of making common cause with the democratic opposition, particularly with the radical Catholics, which they will try to steer towards social revolution after Franco goes. In particular, they have tried to get party members or sympathizers elected to the official syndicates and onto the unofficial factory workers' committees. The Communists, like the Socialists, have suffered from the disruptive action of factions, chiefly on the part of pro-Chinese extremists, and from the strain of following a leadership which has been nearly thirty years in exile. If the party manages to re-emerge, its leaders will probably no longer be the veteran exiles like Santiago Carrillo, its present secretary general, and Dolores Ibárruri ('La Pasionaria'), but unknown men and women who have won their spurs in the underground struggle. Evidence of occasional communist activity inside Spain – though never allowed to reach serious proportions – is probably not unwelcome to a régime which claims credit for having stood, and for still standing, as the great bulwark against the communist menace.

The political pattern of Franco's Spain is thus neither simple nor clear-cut. It does not stand out as an intransigent Government versus an uncompromising Opposition. Much of the picture is a shifting chiaroscuro in which groups and individuals manoeuvre for position, the opposition making accommodations with the régime and using its machinery to gain more elbow-room, the government permitting a certain (though not too dangerous) degree of 'diversification'. Every few years the kaleidoscope has been abruptly shaken: in 1945, when Franco replaced a number of discredited Nazi-Falangist ministers with Christian Democrats; in 1956, when liberal currents, particularly in the universities, provoked sharp Falangist reactions and a general clamp-down by the government; in 1962, when the Asturian miners launched strikes, and scores of opposition leaders left Spain to join monarchist and left-wing leaders in a demonstration of anti-Franco unity at Munich.

The announcement in 1966 of the new Organic Law raised expectations of change to a new pitch. Though the Government claimed that the referendum showed that nearly 96 per cent of the voters favoured Franco's régime, many people no doubt did so because they were economically better off under his rule or because they still looked on him as the best guarantee of law and order or because they believed that his régime was about to liberalize itself. It looked as if the proposed election of more than one hundred 'heads of family' might be the first step towards transforming the Cortes into a really democratic body. The National Movement, too, seemed likely to lose its monopoly of political power.

However, the legislation which followed the Organic Law dashed these hopes. The restrictions placed on the candidates for the Cortes, who were required to swear allegiance to the National Movement, ensured that only supporters of the régime would be returned. Other legislation, by institutionalizing the National Movement, strengthened rather than weakened its grasp of power. The press, which had begun to write more freely after the easing of the censorship in 1966, was overawed by fresh legislation which made it an offence to disseminate news described as 'false', morally harmful, or disrespectful of established legislation. Even the draft legislation extending limited rights to non-Catholics was watered down. A ruling of the supreme court indicated that all strikes were to be considered illegal. The implied promises of more representative labour unions and student bodies and more say in managing their own affairs for Basques and Catalans all remained unfulfilled. Admiral Carrero

Blanco, noted for his unyielding conservatism, was appointed vice-president and emerged as the most powerful figure in the government after General Franco himself. Spain's progress towards a more liberal régime was slowed up, though not entirely halted. The 'heads of family' procuradores at least called attention in the Cortes to some of Spain's pressing economic and social problems. The bishops issued a statement in favour of freer and more representative trade unions enjoying, in certain circumstances, the right to strike. The country thus seemed to be moving to the rhythm of an old Spanish dance; three steps forward, two steps back. No quickening of the pace was clearly to be expected from the man who called the tune. Only the pressure of new social and economic forces and the tenacious struggle of all these elements in the nation who felt the need most keenly still held some promise of change.

NEW ECONOMIC FORCES
The visitor to Madrid, Barcelona, Seville, or any other bustling Spanish city, or to the teeming resorts on the Mediterranean coast, may find it difficult to realize that Spain has not yet worked her passage into the ranks of the fully developed nations. She occupies a place in the intermediate group between developed and undeveloped, and nearer to the latter than to the former. With the exception of Portugal, her average living standards are the lowest in Western Europe. But now, undoubtedly, she is on the move—in a literal sense, to judge from the stream of cars, many of them 'Seats' from her own plant which produce a Spanish version of the Italian Fiat, bearing families to and from their week-end jaunts. The chief beneficiaries of the new prosperity have been the middle classes, hitherto a weak component of Spanish society weighted with small rentiers and civil servants rather than people active in business and trade. The old Castilian indifference to the process of money-making seems to be disappearing, perhaps because energies which formerly went into politics now find a safer outlet in pursuing economic rewards. The majority of middle-class Spaniards, though still exposed to the pinch of inflation and often obliged to take on two or more jobs to make both ends meet, are better dressed and fed than

ever before, and more interested in improving living standards for themselves and their children.

The extraordinary boom in tourism, which has brought the number of foreigners visiting Spain from less than 2 million in 1954 to 17 million in 1966, has not only created new wealth and many new jobs in Spain, but cannot have failed to help imbue Spaniards with modern European attitudes which take comfortable living standards for granted. Some of this increasing prosperity – and certainly the demand for better material conditions – is seeping down to the workers, though here the repressive hand of official labour regimentation still lies heavy. By and large, however, the lot of the industrial worker has improved and the minimum wage (raised to 102 pesetas a day in January 1969) represents not only a reflection of the cost of living, which has risen 28 per cent in the last three years, but an improvement, if only a slight one, in real terms. The best way, however, for a worker to earn money is to go abroad and join the many who find work in other countries and whose remittances form a useful contribution to Spain's foreign currency receipts.

The Spain of which Franco first found himself master a was land devastated by wars, its roads and railways shattered, its factories idle and its fields deserted, the population decimated and divided. Recovery was slow, lagging far behind that of a Germany visited by an even more terrible destruction. Partly this was due to the isolation of Franco's régime; shunned by the western democracies and finding little help from the Axis powers who were concentrating their resources for the coming war, Spain could not obtain the aid and trade necessary for her recovery. After the war, when the Marshall Plan began to lift Western Europe back to prosperity, she still found herself left to one side. Nor were the people (except in Catalonia and the Basque provinces) noted for the sort of entrepreneurial skill and dogged industriousness which was necessary if a country was to be put back on its feet. Spain was left to stagnate under the weight of its traditional disabilities: an intractable, fragmented geography, an antiquated communications system, a neglected agriculture, a lack of basic requirements for economic development such as petroleum and high-grade coal, and a falling off in the production of certain minerals, such as copper and lead, which had once been a source of wealth.

Franco approached his country's ills as a soldier, not as an economist. Spain was isolated; then she must make a virtue of necessity and look to herself for salvation. This meant a policy of regimentation, of autarchy and state controls, of pegged prices and wages and limitation of imports. Consequently, Spain's industrial production was slow to pick up, and it was not for a decade and a half that she again reached preCivil War levels. The chosen instrument for 'the development of our economic autarchy' was a state development corporation, the Instituto Nacional de Industria (INI) headed by Juan Antonio Suanzes, a naval engineer and longtime friend of the Caudillo. By the mid'fifties, INI had grown into a vast industrial empire owning or controlling scores of enterprises – the spectacular new steel works at Avilés, near Oviedo, shipyards, mines and oil refineries, power and fertilizer plants, aircraft and automobile factories, and other key industries. Thanks to its privileged position – for the corporation was financed for many years out of the national budget, and then by means of loans from the state bank at specially favourable rates – INI made notable headway in such fields as engineering, metallurgy, chemicals and electric energy (which doubled in the course of a decade). Nevertheless, the price paid for the wastefulness of many of the giant's multifarious operations was high. Spain found herself impelled towards an inflationary spiral which was to have farreaching social and economic consequences.

The brunt of these inflationary pressures was borne by the workers. Regimented in a series of 'vertical' *sindicatos* grouping together labour, management and government representatives, they were caught between rising prices and a fixed wage structure and had no effective means of bargaining for better conditions. The assumption underlying the régime's conception of labour relations was that there should be no strikes by the workers and no dismissals by management, and that the government would provide a wide range of services in the form of sickness and retirement benefits, housing projects, welfare schemes and so on. Nevertheless, these benefits could be withheld at will, and no strike fund existed for the support of recalcitrant workers. As inflation mounted and worker discontent grew, the Falangist bosses – who had reasons of their own for causing embarrass-ment to their conservative and monarchist partners in 'the Movement' – decided to break with established policy and pressed for the grant-ing of an all-round increase in wages. The increase was authorized in 1956, but because management was precluded from making economies by dismissing redundant staff and no increase in produc-tivity resulted from the higher wage scale, prices continued to rise, necessitating further salary increases and leading to the acceleration of inflation. A mounting current of labour unrest followed and the workers continued to demand higher wages and unions more genuinely representative of their interests, with leaders elected from below rather than imposed from above. However, labour dis-content still smoulders and constitutes the most sustained, though not always apparent, challenge to the Franco régime. To by-pass the official sindicatos, 'workers' commissions' have come into existence. Though many of their leaders have been jailed and the commissions themselves are regarded as illegal, they meet in public and, since they are principally concerned with genuine labour objectives and not politics, the government is finding it increasingly difficult to ignore them. In the official sindicatos, too, more authentic representatives of the workers – often men of socialist, Christian Democrat or communist conviction – are getting elected. The leaders are still nominated by the régime, but such men as José Solís, Minister and Secretary of the Falange as well as supreme boss of the sindicatos, have tried to improve their image as genuine labour leaders with the interests of the workers at heart, and have worked hard to gain for Spain's still corporate-type syndicates a greater degree of acceptance in the international trade union movement.

There were other factors too which made the 'fifties a crucial period in Spain's economic development. In 1953, she moved out of her traditional isolation to the extent of signing an important agree-ment with the United States for the construction of bases and the supply of military aid. The following year the first shipments of important non-military aid began to reach Spain. Less than one-third of this aid was in the form of food-stuffs (thereby saving Spain much-needed foreign currency), a slightly larger amount in raw materials for her new factories, and over one-third in capital equipment and machinery. American aid certainly helped Spain to sustain the industrial boom of the 'fifties; whether it also contributed to her inflationary troubles is another matter. By 1957, the continual rise in prices, worsening balance of trade, and the fall in Spain's gold reserves had become sufficiently serious to cause Franco to replace his Falangist ministers by a new economic team, most of them associated with the Opus Dei movement. Despite the efforts of these 'technocrats' to curb the overheated economy, the demands made on the national budget by military expenditure and by INI's lavish schemes, together with a lagging agriculture and the investment by wealthy Spaniards of money in other European countries, were leading to a disastrous drop in the value of the peseta and the exhaustion of the gold reserves. Spain was on the brink of bankruptcy. Realizing that its stability would be threatened by an economic crash, the Spanish government reluctantly heeded the advice of foreign experts who had been urging a policy of retrenchment. After consultations with the Organization for European Economic Cooperation, the World Bank, the International Monetary Fund and other authorities, Franco realized that there was no alternative to the introduction of a period of austerity, and in mid-1959 the Government announced its stabilization plan. Once again it was the workers who felt the pinch most keenly. In 1962, the Asturian miners came out on strike and faced Franco's régime with its most serious challenge since his accession to power.

After this painful period of restraint, measures were needed to reflate the economy on a sounder, more balanced basis. Franco's new technocrats – the economist Alberto Ullastres, López Rodó, a professor of administrative law, banker Navarro Rubio, and their colleagues – set about elaborating a national plan which incorporated many of the proposals previously made by the foreign experts. The opinions of a number of leading figures from Spanish industrial, financial and commercial interests were called in for consultation. This in itself was something of an innovation; it denoted, if not a true democratization of the régime (for the authentic voice of Labour was still silent) at least a gesture on the part of the régime to associate a wider cross-section of the nation with the processes of governmental planning.

At the beginning of 1964, the Government launched its plan for economic and social development – the first attempt in Spanish history to put forward an integrated programme of regional develop-ment and economic expansion for the entire nation. Strongly influ-enced by French planning techniques, the plan was conceived as a cooperative effort between state and private initiative, which fixed goals obligatory for the former but only indicative for the latter: an annual increase in the gross national product of 6 per cent, a rise of 10 per cent in exports, 11 per cent in proceeds from tourism and 9 per cent in capital investment. Foreign investment was welcomed and provision made for the free remittance of profits and repatriation of capital. Most of the capital investment was aimed at the improve-ment of Spain's transport system, housing and urbanization, agri-culture and irrigation projects, education and vocational training. It was to be primarily channelled, by means of a system of tax incen-tives and other fiscal advantages, to seven 'industrial growth and development zones' – Burgos, Valladolid, Saragossa, Vigo, Seville, Corunna and Huelva.

How successful has Spain's first plan been? Some decried or opposed it from the outset: the intransigent Falangists who believed in the subordination of economics to politics and saw in it the aban-donment of their cherished autarchist aims; businessmen who had thrived on high-cost production in a protected market and feared the effects of liberalization and competition; xenophobes who protested that greedy foreign capitalists would now be free to suck away Spain's life-blood. Nevertheless economic development there has certainly been; not the orderly progress foreseen by the planners, but a lurching forward, uncertainly and sometimes dangerously, with balance of payments troubles, and the government applying anti-inflationary measures by restricting credit but unable to cut down its own un-productive expenditure. The annual rate of economic growth has sometimes fluctuated to 8 instead of 6 per cent, but productivity has consistently lagged behind consumption. *Per capita* income has risen

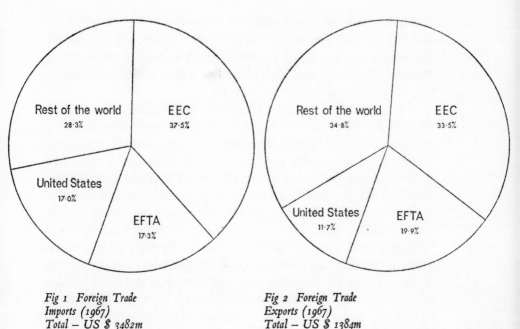

Fig 1 Foreign Trade
Imports (1967)
Total – US $ 3482m

Fig 2 Foreign Trade
Exports (1967)
Total – US $ 1384m

*Source: Economist (Spanish language edition, 12 June 1968. Vol 2 No 12) and Ministry of Trade

from $448 in 1963 to over $700 in 1967, yet the country continues to export too little and import too much. The government has found itself without the necessary resources to stimulate economic growth in all the specified zones of development. Foreign capital continues to flow in, but lack of adequate roads, housing facilities and other services, which the government should provide, discourage foreign investment there. Nor has this situation been helped by the present uncertainty regarding Spain's chances of getting into the Common Market. Most serious of all, by the end of the first Four Year Plan, prices were rising faster in Spain than anywhere else in Western Europe. A writer in the newspaper El Alcázar calculated that if a worker bought a dozen eggs, it would cost him an hour's work in Spain, 24 minutes in France and 8 in Britain; a litre of milk would cost him 17 minutes' work in Spain, but only 9 in France or Britain; and if he should aim as high as a car, he would need to work the equivalent of 2,682 hours in Spain, 1,666 in France and 1,000 in Britain. The 'Spanish miracle' was thus a long way from satisfying the expectations at least of the workers.

The Second Development Plan (1968–71) should help to correct some of the short-comings of the first and also profit from the boost to exports expected from the devaluation of the peseta which followed closely upon that of the pound. Where the first plan emphasized overall growth, the second stresses the principle of selectivity and has allocated half the total funds proposed to the still deficient sectors of transport and agriculture. In the case of the latter, an annual growth rate in productivity of 5·5 per cent is the target; Spain's excessive and high-cost production of cereals is to be cut by reducing the wheat crop; the use of tractors, fertilizers and insecticides is to be stepped up, as are schemes for irrigation and reafforestation; the consolidation of small-holdings is to be extended; and an attempt will be made to raise the agricultural worker's income so that it will be nearer to that of the national average. Education is also to be expanded and three new universities built. Will these admirable and much needed measures stand any chance of proving effective without upsetting the structural problems of Spain's economy with all their explosive social and political implications? The land question has deep roots in Spain's past and raises difficult and fundamental issues.

THE LAND PROBLEM
This is in reality not one problem, but a whole complex of inter-related problems stemming from the diversity of historical and social conditions, types of agriculture and systems of land tenure to be found throughout Spain. But the main contours are clear enough. Firstly, there is the disastrously low level of productivity. Though there has been an industrial expansion of 73 per cent in the last five years, agriculture continues to stagnate, food prices rise and the pressure of inflation increases. Agriculture still accounts for nearly 20 per cent of Spain's gross national product and for half her exports. Yet she is increasingly unable to feed herself and needs to import

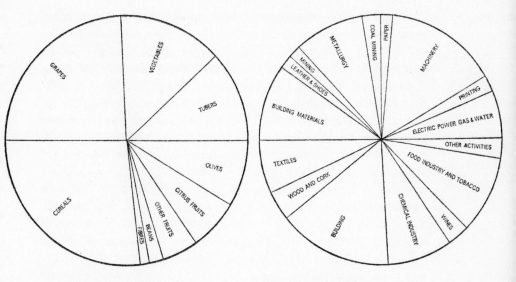

Fig 3 Agricultural Production   Fig 4 Industrial Production

*Source: Ministries of Agriculture and Industry 1966

more and more food – for example, by 1965 food imports were costing more than the value of the food exported. About 30 per cent of Spain's active population is today engaged in agriculture. At the beginning of the century, nearly two-thirds of the country's inhabitants lived from agriculture. By 1930, the proportion had fallen to nearly 46 per cent. It rose again in the lean years following the Civil War but since the Second World War it has dropped as the nation has grown generally more prosperous, though there are immense variations in the different parts of the country. In Catalonia, for instance, the proportion engaged in agriculture has already declined to 12·5 and is expected to reach 8 per cent by 1970. In the depressed provinces of central and southern Spain, the bulk of the inhabitants (77 per cent in Orense, 72 per cent in Avila and Toledo, 71 per cent in Badajoz) still strive to draw their living from an ailing agriculture.

From this there follows another striking feature of Spain's land problem: the intolerable poverty of the rural population. Here again, of course, we find wide regional variations. The small-holder in the Basque provinces may hope for a reasonable livelihood, but the owner of a Galician dwarf-holding, or – in still more desperate plight – the landless labourer of Andalusia, barely subsists above the starvation level. One cannot help wondering whether the food the Andalusian bracero eats really can produce the 2,746 which was reckoned to be the average calorie intake in 1963, and which the development plan set out to raise to over 3,000 by the end of 1967. The food with which the *patrón* supplies the bracero is almost invariably *gazpacho*, a soup made of tomatoes, oil, vinegar and water, with pieces of bread floating in it, which is delicious when served ice-cold as the first course in a good restaurant, but which the bracero takes hot for breakfast, cold for lunch and hot again for his supper. The bracero's employment is only seasonal. For six months of the year he remains idle. This is not because he is idle by nature. 'The peasants of no country upon earth are more patient of heat, of hunger and of thirst, or capable of greater exertions than this very people who have been accused of indolence', wrote an English traveller in the eighteenth century.[32] The huge estates, wholly given over to an in-different wheat crop, need his labour only at sowing and harvest-time. The landowner himself is an absentee who entrusts his land to a bailiff or leases it to a tenant. He sees no reason to waste his capital on its improvement, for he can live comfortably in Madrid or Seville on its rent and on the guaranteed prices the state pays for his cereals. Between the landowner and his illiterate or semi-illiterate braceros there yawns a gulf of economic, social and cultural differences, of fear and scorn on the one side, of hatred and envy on the other. The braceros are not only exploited; they know they are exploited. Before the Civil War their resentment found vent in passionate anarchism. Now they protest, more often than not, simply by leaving the great estates.

The origin of the large estates lies in that phase of the Reconquest when the armies of King Alfonso VI captured Toledo and penetra-

136

ted deep into al-Andalus. Hitherto, territory taken from the Moors had remained at the disposal of those who had conquered and could work it. The northern part of the peninsula thus came to be divided up into small and medium-sized farms which in the course of time frequently became fragmented into the dwarf-holdings or *minifundia* of today. But in the centre and south of Spain, the more recently conquered lands were given by the Crown to the Church, the religious orders and the great nobles who were better able to organize their rehabilitation and defence. Nineteenth-century liberal legislation disentailed the great estates, many of which, together with land owned by the Church or held by the municipalities, passed into the hands of a new class of landowners. The pueblos lost almost all the land they traditionally held in common and a new rural proletariat of braceros was brought into being. The outcome has been the vast disproportion – unique in Europe – between the few who own enormous areas of land and the many who have small plots or nothing at all. A recent survey shows that whilst five million of those who have land in Spain own an average of no more than 1 hectare, 51,283 owners between them own over half of the land, or 446 hectares per head. The accumulation of estates by inheritance and marriage can endow the great landowning families with patrimonies of astronomical size which are reflected in their multiple titles of nobility. The Duchess of Medinaceli, for instance, is also Duchess of Camiña, Ciudad Real, Denia, Santisteban del Puerto, Segorbe and Tarifa; *Marquesa* de Alcalá de la Alameda, Aytona, Cogolludo, Comares, Malagón, Montalbán, Navahermosa, Las Navas, Pallars, Priego, Solera, Tarifa, La Torrecilla, Villa Real, Villalba; *condesa* of Alcoutim, Ampurias, Aramayona, Beundía, Castellar de la Fron- tera, Cocentaina, Medellín, Los Molares, Ofalla, Osuna, Prades, Del Riscó, Santa Gadea, Velenza y Valladares and Villalonso; *vizcondesa* of Cabrera, Bas, Linares and Villamur.[33]

The necessity of reforming this lopsided and antiquated agrarian structure has long been realized and various schemes have been put forward from the time of Jovellanos, the great exponent of eighteenth- century enlightenment. But not until the Second Republic was a resolute onslaught made on the problem. The Land Reform Law of 1932 proposed the expropriation of all land belonging to the Grandees, of any land left uncultivated or badly cultivated by their owners and of other estates owned above a specified size which varied according to local conditions. The grandees were to get no compensation; the other dispossessed owners were to be paid partly in bonds and partly in cash. Despite its defects and obscurities – it was to be left to 'communities of peasants' to decide whether to work their new land individually or collectively – the Land Reform Law could have changed the whole face of Spain. But implementation was delayed, and a start had only just been made on carrying it into effect when the Civil War broke out. One of the first acts of the National Government at Burgos was to declare the Land Reform Law suspended (18 August 1936). It is true that there was subsequently placed on the statute book a law of 1953 relating to 'Farms manifestly capable of improvement' which could be expropriated if the improvements needed were not carried out. However, this has remained virtually a dead letter. In theory, some small tenants are entitled to profit from the government-sponsored irrigation schemes. But by and large, the whole problem of agrarian reform has been shelved. As one well-informed authority has said, Franco's failure to tackle it is not surprising. 'He has, it is true, put some pressure on the large landlords to bring their waste and fallow lands under cultivation and in general to make more effective use of their properties. He could hardly go further without alienating a power group that is one of his principal supports.'[34]

The Government has made more headway with the problem of the minifundia. The classic land of the dwarf-holdings is Galicia, where the countryside is dotted with tiny farms barely capable of supporting a single family. The average size of each farm is 3·6 hectares, split up into 16·5 minute plots. The government has passed a number of laws to deal with the problem engendered by these dwarf-holdings, the first (1952) establishing a Land Consolidation Service which, with the help of U.S. funds, has done valuable work. But the proportions of the problem are gigantic, since it is reckoned that as much as eight million hectares of land stand in need of consolidation and that, at the present rate of progress, it would take eighty years to solve the problem! Moreover, the Land Consolidation Service is only empowered to re-arrange the existing holdings of the respective owners; it cannot touch the thorny political question of redistributing the land between those who have too little and those who have a surplus. Though all landowners benefit from the operation of consolidation, the larger landowners benefit most, since the smallholders may still not have enough land to be able to benefit from mechanization and other improved techniques. Perhaps some improvement could result from the cooperative working of consolidated holdings. The initiative in this direction has already been taken in Navarre, where the Municipality of Santa María de Zúñiga, which previously comprised 310 hectares of land split up into 218 plots held by 45 owners, first had these holdings consolidated and then decided to work them on a cooperative basis. The results were striking: a 28 per cent increase in productivity in a single year.[35] The Ministry of Agriculture at first looked at this initiative with some misgiving, fearing that it might be the thin end of the wedge of 'collectivization'. However, neighbouring municipalities have been quick to see its advantages and to apply for similar consolidation and communal operation. Navarre, it is true, is a region where farming is relatively prosperous, but it is also one noted for its extreme conservatism. If a system of cooperative working – but not of cooperative ownership of land – succeeds in establishing itself in the north of Spain as the most hopeful answer to the problem of the minifundia, may it not also point the way to the still more difficult problem of the latifundia, once there is a régime in Spain which is prepared to face this fundamental issue?

Other measures which deal with the problem of agricultural stagnation include reafforestation and soil conservation schemes, provision for more fertilizers and tractors, and, above all, an ambitious programme of irrigation works. In her agriculture, as in so much else, Spain is a country of striking contrasts. Less than 9 per cent of her farmland is at present irrigated, but this relatively small area of very fertile land provides one-third of all her agricultural produce and more than half her agricultural exports. In the vegas of Andalusia and the Levante, where irrigation makes possible two or even three crops a year, yields are four to six times higher than from unirrigated land in the same climate. The first development plan concentrated on the construction of dams and irrigation networks, with the aim of bringing 300,000 hectares under irrigation within the four-year period. Though some of the results achieved, as in the formerly barren areas round Badajoz and Jaén, are impressive, the cost has been enormous and progress slow. Experts calculate that the total area of land in Spain capable of being irrigated amounts to five million hectares, and that at the present rate the task would not be completed until well after the year 2000. Here again, as with so many of the reforms sponsored by the Franco régime, one must pause to ask who are the chief beneficiaries. In 1939, an Instituto Nacional de Colonisación was established in order to settle *colonos* on the newly irrigated lands. Within the first twenty-five years of its existence, this institute has settled no more than a modest average of 2,000 colonos a year. For not all the land selected for irrigation is distributed amongst former tenants or landless labourers. The law permits the owner of a latifundio to retain a proportion, calculated according to the size of his family and other factors and averaging nearly three-quarters of the area to be irrigated.[36] Irrigation brings benefits to the few fortunate colonos and, in still larger measure, to the large landowner who, 'thanks to the transformation of the land reserved for his use, may manage to double or treble his net income, whilst at the same time receiving a substantial sum in cash for the unirrigated land expro-priated from him.'[37]

Irrigation, by making possible a more diversified type of farming capable of keeping a colono regularly occupied instead of subject to the long spells of seasonal unemployment inseparable from cereal monoculture, may also help to alleviate one of Spain's most serious problems: the flight from the land. Throughout her long history, Spain has suffered from phases of rural depopulation and emigration: the strife between Moors and Christians, the drain on Castilian man-power through European wars and the conquest and colonization of the New World, the emigration by which men sought to escape from the turmoil and exhaustion of the nineteenth century. The pre-sent exodus is largely due to the prospect of better opportunities and higher wages either abroad, in labour-scarce Germany, France and Belgium, or in great cities like Madrid and Barcelona, the zones of industrial development, or the booming tourist resorts of the Mediterranean coast. Kept within bounds, this shift of population is both natural and beneficial, for we have noted that Spain still has too high a proportion of its people (although it has been falling) engaged in agriculture. Since 1964, the exodus has become a stampede. *Campesinos* leave the land at the rate of a quarter of a million every year, and not only from those regions like Galicia and Andalusia where some degree of emigration is traditional, but also from Castile and La Mancha, where the peasant is more deeply rooted to his land. Eighteen out of Spain's fifty provinces, which together account for a quarter of her population and nearly 45 per cent of her land area, are now being drained of their life-blood. In Soria, Guadalajara and Albacete one finds whole villages falling into ruin, the schools closed for lack of pupils, and totally deserted except for a handful of old people. The young and enterprising have left the unpaved streets and unlit homes in search of better things, even if it is only to land up in the squalid shanty-towns which now ring the large cities. Where will this process stop, and what can be done about it? Is Spain heading for a state of affairs where the towns and fertile vegas will be no more than oases set amidst vast stretches of semi-desert? Even the forty new villages constructed under the Badajoz scheme represent little more than a marginal improvement, for the problem is now assuming the proportions of a demographic revolution. Few would go to the opposite extreme of advocating that the exodus should be arrested by dotting the country indiscriminately with factories. Industry must continue to develop, especially if it is a question of attracting private capital, where a good economic infrastructure and labour supply already exist. But means must also be found for rehabilitating the residual population of the countryside by making conditions there more tolerable and for providing alternative prospects of employment. One useful measure would be the establishment of regional development boards which could not only call on the resources of the central government but tap the deep reserves of local pride and initiative. This, however, would lead straight to another intractable complex of problems which the government refuses to face: the age-old tension between heartland and periphery, between centralism and regionalism, between the urge for local autonomy and the fear of separatism and national disintegration.

THE REGIONAL PROBLEM

The official view does not recognize the existence of any such prob-lem. Franco's Spain is a unitary, centralized state permitting no regional particularity or local government in which regional initia-tive, interests and attitudes might have free play. All important decisions are made in Madrid. Though Franco himself is a Gallego, Castilian officials, or other Spaniards who share the official centrali-zing philosophy, administer the country. Regional autonomy has become identified with the Republic. The great centres of regionalist sentiment such as Barcelona and Bilbao, which were also great Republican strongholds during the Civil War, have been slowest to reconcile themselves to Franco's rule. Beneath the surface of enforced uniformity, there still remains a Catalan question, a Basque question, even a Galician question. Autonomist sentiment cannot express it-self in political terms, but centres instead around those basic cultural and educational issues which have always nurtured it. Thus the Catalans stubbornly demand for their children the right to be taught Catalan in their schools, and the régime, which still bans Catalan newspapers and has only grudgingly permitted the publication of books in Catalan, as stubbornly refuses. Whilst the old battle of the class-rooms rages, new social and economic forces are at work reshaping the regional problems in directions which cannot always be predicted. What will be the outcome of the immigration into Catalonia and the Basque provinces of hundreds of thousands of Castilian-speaking labourers from Murcia, Andalusia and Estre-madura? Will it dilute the traditional character of the region and help to Castilianize it, or will the children of these immigrants grow up to speak and think as Catalans and Basques, in areas which feel themselves to be less 'Spanish', but which are growing more populous and more prosperous than other parts of Spain? And what if Spain moves closer, as it seems she must, to an ever more integrated Europe? The Catalans have always prided themselves on being more 'European' than Castilians or Andalusians. Others challenge this view; the intense individualism and clannishness of the Catalonians, they argue, is in reality a sign that the Catalans are essentially Spanish. 'The Catalan out-Spaniards the Spaniard in many ways', concludes Salvador Madariaga, 'and far from being a European exiled in an African Spain, he is an Iberian showing some of the typical Iberian features more markedly than the other Peninsular peoples'.[38]

The roots of the Catalan question stretch back deep into Spanish history, where each side claims to find ample evidence to prove its respective case. The centralist points to the steady coalescing of small into larger units, the inevitable extension to the periphery of the coordinating control of the centre. First, Asturias and Galicia merge into Leon, then Leon with Castile; in the east, Catalonia merges with Aragon and then Aragon with Castile, culminating in the unity and greatness of Spain. This unity should not be seen as uniformity, but as a partnership in which each retains distinctive individuality and institutions. Any move to upset the delicate balance – so the argument runs – in the name of greater 'autonomy' would lead inevitably to the weakening and disruption of the common Spanish state. So Castile was justified in suppressing the great Catalan revolt of 1640 and in storming a defiant Barcelona in 1714. As Primo de Rivera, who attempted to arrest the revived trend towards autonomy by imposing a stern centralist régime in 1923, put it: 'to reconstitute a region, to strengthen its individuality, to encourage the pride with which one region differentiates itself from another, is to contribute towards the destruction of the great work of national unity.'[39]

Very different are the conclusions which the Catalan nationalist draws from his country's history. First, he will recall with pride its brilliant achievements in the Middle Ages; the poetry of the troubadours, the romantic life and vast literary output of the missionary-mystic Ramón Lull, the diffusion of Catalan language, culture and institutions by Catalan-Aragonese merchants, soldiers and administrators throughout the Mediterranean. Then, after centuries of decline and the denationalizing policy of the Bourbon kings, the

remarkable *renaixensa* of the nineteenth century: a linguistic and liter/
ary revival first, leading to a growing political demand, though the
issue was confused by anarchist and Marxist revolutionary cross/
currents, for political autonomy. With the proclamation of the First
Republic, the federalists seemed to have a solution within their grasp.
But the restoration of the monarchy renewed the tug/of/war between
Madrid and Barcelona. Was it just, the Catalans complained, that
because their country was more industrious and progressive, it should
be bled by intolerable taxation to support the indolence and back/
wardness of other parts of Spain? Deprived by Primo de Rivera's
dictatorship of all constitutional means of furthering their aspirations,
some Catalans, under the nationalist leader Francesc Maciá, actually
attempted an abortive invasion from France in a bid to set up an
independent Catalan state. Home rule, however, rather than separat/
ism has been the goal of Catalan nationalists, and this goal was for a
time actually achieved under the Statute of Autonomy during the
brief and troubled life of the Second Republic. Under the Franco
administration the pendulum has swung back again towards central/
ism. During the last thirty years enough incidents have occurred, such
as the demonstrations in favour of the Catalan flag during the Caud/
illo's visit to Barcelona in 1960, to make it clear that Catalan national/
ism is only dormant. Madrid, however, still holds the whip hand and
is not slow, whenever there are signs of serious disaffection, to crack
her whip.

The Basque question resembles the Catalan in certain respects,
though it has features of its own. The Basques, too, are prosperous
and industrious folk who resent what they deem to be the exploitation
and disregard of their national individuality by the central power.
The possession of a totally dissimilar language, they claim, betokens
their distinctive race and the right to run their own affairs. The use of
the Basque tongue – unlike that of Catalan – now appears to be
receding. It is little spoken in the chief towns of the region, and its
difference and extraordinary complexity make it difficult for immi/
grants to acquire. Though the language is rich in folk poetry, and the
improvised verse duels known as *bertsolaris* still draw audiences in
Guipúzcoa, the Basques have no legacy of written literature. Nor

indeed can they look back to the political ideal of a united Basque state. Basque nationalism is a late nineteenth-century creation. Its founder was Sabino Arana Goiri (b. 1865) who studied at Barcelona where the influence of Catalan nationalism led him to found a movement for which he coined the name Euzkadi (Basque Fatherland) and the slogan 'God and the old laws!' The Second Republic brought to the Basques, as to the Catalans, a brief taste of autonomy which was extinguished with the victory of Franco. The restoration of their chartered rights remains the programme of the Basque nationalists, though it is far from clear how the fueros of a century and a half ago could be made to fit modern conditions. Perhaps they would settle for a return to the *Concierto Económico*, an arrangement by which the Basque provinces were taxed an agreed lump sum which they could raise amongst themselves as they saw fit. Most Basques would probably agree with the spokesman who wrote recently, 'A return to the régime of fueros would be a perfect solution to the Basque problem, and one which would also satisfy those who are not Basques but sincerely wish to see the problem solved.'[40] This certainly falls short of the demands of the Basque Nationalist Party (PNV), which maintains a 'government in exile' in Paris, and of the more militant ETA (Euzkadi Ta Askatatuna – Basque Fatherland and Freedom). The latter combines separatism with an extreme Left programme and believes in direct action. A series of terrorist acts, culminating in the assassination by the ETA of the secret police chief for Guipúzcoa, led in 1968 to the proclamation of a state of emergency and shows that nationalism is still an explosive force in Spanish politics.

Is there also a *problema gallego* – a problem of Galicia? There is certainly, as we have seen, a problem of rural overpopulation, poverty and emigration, but is there also a national problem analogous to that of the Basques and Catalans? The Republic seems to have been in two minds about this, since it gave Galicia only the promise and not the substance of autonomy. The *gallego* who is today the master of a centralized Spain permits no doubt about the answer, and instead of autonomy holds out the prospects of economic progress stemming from the two 'poles of development' at Vigo and

Corunna. Nor can the Galicians console themselves with the hope that their cultural identity, which contributed such splendid poetry during the Middle Ages and again in the last century, will receive much official encouragement. The University of Santiago de Compostela, around which a distinctive regional culture might be expected to develop, languishes. This mist-enshrouded corner of Spain remains an Iberian Wales deprived of its Eisteddfod, lest her people come to look with too much sympathy to their Portuguese cousins beyond the border whom they resemble so much in speech and racial origins.

6   Traditional attitudes and new trends

THE REGIONAL QUESTION interlocks – as so many other issues still do in Spain – with that of the Catholic Church. We have noted the dominant role played by the Church in forging the unity and greatness of Spain, and how it then became a buttress of the old order against the new liberal currents, finally losing altogether its hold over the poorer classes. Only in certain parts of Spain, notably in the Basque provinces, where those classes remained fiercely attached to their ancient traditions, did the country clergy continue to voice popular aspirations and become the champions both of conservatism and of regional nationalism. Elsewhere the masses, particularly the industrial workers, turned to the creeds of anarchism, and later to socialism and communism, and regarded the Church as ranged against them on the side of their privileged oppressors.

Anti-clericalism – a phenomenon familiar enough elsewhere in Europe – attained in Spain a particular ferocity, and vented itself periodically in the burning down of convents and churches and the murder of priests, monks and nuns, as in the horrifying excesses of Barcelona's 'Tragic Week' of 1909. With the coming of the Second Republic anti-clericalism became official policy. The fanatical intoler-ance which the Catholic Church had so often shown against its enemies was turned against the Church itself. Religious orders were forbidden to teach or to own property and the Jesuits were expelled. The Republic, it seemed, was bent on uprooting Catholicism itself. Franco was thus able to convince those who still cherished the ancient faith that, in taking up arms to oppose the Republic, he was acting in defence of religion. A pastoral letter, signed in 1937 by all but three of the bishops in Spain, ranged the hierarchy firmly behind the rebel movement. The victory of the Caudillo was proclaimed a victory for the Church. For the last thirty years, whatever reservations some churchmen may express about it, the Church as a whole has remained deeply identified with his régime.

Franco has sought to restore the close partnership between Church and State which was the traditional basis for the nation's greatness. The Republic's anti-clerical legislation was at once repealed, the Orders were invited to resume their work, and the Church was given wide influence over education and the media of publicity. The relationship was formalized in the Concordat of 1953 which confirmed the privileges of the Church, ensured financial support for it from the State, but accorded the latter a large measure of control over ecclesiastical affairs by reserving to the head of state the right to 'present' candidates for episcopal appointment. As an institution, the Church has clearly gained tremendously in terms of power and prestige from its close association with the régime. In return, it has lent to the latter an aura of respectability and legitimacy. Nevertheless, the Church has not been allowed a monopoly of influence; it must share power with the Falange, which contains strong anti-clerical elements. Cardinal Pla, the Spanish Primate, endeavoured in vain to induce General Franco to grant more effective powers to the Catholic workingmen's associations, the *Hermandades Obreras de Acción Católica* (HOAC), at the expense of the Falangist-controlled *sindicatos*. The Vatican itself is now believed to be pressing for a revision of the 1953 Concordat, particularly in respect of the head of state's 'right of presentation' which would make it easier for Rome to appoint younger bishops whose outlook is more in sympathy with that of the Vatican Council.

Though the church hierarchy remains on the whole conservative, it would be wrong to think of Spain as dominated today by 'clerical reaction'; still less can one speak of it as a 'priest-ridden' country. Such a description might have been appropriate two hundred years ago when there was one priest to every 140 of the population, or even in the middle of the last century, when the proportion was still one in every 400. Today there are about 25,000 priests in Spain –

about one priest to every 1,200 of the population, which is no more than the average for western Europe as a whole and less than in such countries as France, Italy and Ireland. The proportion varies widely according to region and the 'religious' map of Spain would look (except for Galicia, which is materially poor, though rich in priests) remarkably like the country's economic map. The more prosperous north and north-east is also the part where the ratio of priest to population is highest (one to five hundred); the poor and backward south has relatively fewer priests (one to every two or three thousand). These figures do not suggest any direct correlation between poverty and priest-ridden piety. If we look more closely at the picture, we shall find that although more priests are at work in those wealthier regions, a high proportion of them originate in the poorer regions, particularly from peasant families. The age-structure of the clergy also shows anomalies. There is a marked shortage of priests now in the higher middle-age groups. During the Civil War, between four and five thousand priests are believed to have been killed and neither during that period, nor in the preceding troubled years of the Republic, were there many religious vocations. Following the Civil War, however, when religious fervour reached a new height and the Church again offered an attractive career, so many young men entered the priesthood that there resulted a sort of 'religious inflation'. In the last decade, however, this has gradually given way to a relative 'recession'. There is a great cleavage in outlook between the older, pre-Civil War generation of priests (the average age of the 80 cardinals, archbishops and bishops who make up the Spanish Episcopal Conference is nearly 68, whilst the late Primate was over ninety) and the younger priests whose minds are more open to the fresh winds reaching Spain after the Second Vatican Council. Moreover, the pattern of recruitment is changing. As the rural population diminishes in relation to the nation's total population and an increasingly wide choice of employment is opened up to young people, so the number of vocations from peasant families declines and that from the middle classes begins to rise. This situation may tend to ensure that those who do choose to become priests are more in touch with the outlook and background of their parishioners.

The teaching activities of the Church are mostly carried out by the Orders, which also wield great influence in many other spheres of national life. Some Abbots sit in the Cortes and have the rank of grandees, though some, such as the former Abbot of the famous Catalan monastery of Montserrat, have been notable for their opposition to the régime. The Jesuits, who less than fifty years ago were estimated to control one-third of the whole capital wealth of Spain, remain a powerful if now less obtrusive force.[41] A certain tension between the Orders and the secular clergy can sometimes be noted. In a recent study of a Madrid parish it was observed that 'the parish church has not become the social centre it is, for example, in England. In the main the people have preferred the monks as confessors, advisers, family friends and mediators'. One reason for this is that monks 'take their vows of poverty and live in disciplined communities maintained by funds derived from their teaching and cultural activities, from donations and from the richer religious houses of America. They have therefore no pressing need to earn money from purely religious services, unlike the secular clergy who often live with their families and engage in business as a sideline. The parishioner is not slow to draw comparisons'.[42]

To the great Orders which Spain has given to the Church – the Dominicans, the Jesuits, and the Mercedarians – she has now added a controversial newcomer – the Opus Dei. Founded by a Spanish lawyer and university teacher, José María Escrivá, now a monsignor resident in Rome, the Order made slow headway until after the Civil War, when its adherents amongst the professional classes – doctors, engineers, lawyers, architects, economists, bankers and university teachers – began to play a role of national importance in what they see as the re-christianization of Spain. To its enemies the Order is a sinister form of 'white masonry', which they dub the 'Octopus Dei'. Though its leadership includes both priests and laymen, the strength of Opus Dei lies primarily in its lay character – the abilities and devotion of the 'technocrats' who are believed to include such top planners in the government as López Rodó and Ullastres. The Order is said to run the Banco Popular and many other important financial institutions and to back two of Madrid's daily papers. It has made a special impact on higher education, challenging Falangist influence in the universities and founding a new university of its own at Pamplona. In the influence which it exercises in high places, in its concern for education, its economic resources, its efficiency and the aura of secrecy surrounding its operations, Opus Dei inevitably recalls the Jesuits in their heyday. Will this Order become for a new Catholic revival what the Society of Jesus was for the Counter-Reformation? The virtues enjoined in its founder's book *Camino* are the classic features of Spanish Catholicism – militancy and obedience, coupled with a more novel stress on discretion, humility and good humour. The Order's leaders disclaim any concerted political line. Some members are believed to favour an authoritarian monarchy under Don Juan Carlos, others a liberal monarchy under Don Juan. Opus Dei is certainly no manifestation of the Catholic Left. It wants to see a Spain modernized, but still nourished from its Catholic roots and cautiously integrated into a progressive but politically conservative Western Europe. The role which, with the Vatican's blessing, it has assigned to itself is that of a dedicated intermediary between the traditional Orders, born in a different age and for different purposes, and the rather amorphous mass organizations such as Catholic Action.[43]

Catholic Action, with a membership of about half a million, is recognized by the Concordat as the arm through which the Church chiefly conducts its 'apostolate'. At the local level, its 'militants' are organized into men's and women's groups which cooperate with the parish priest in such matters as promoting compliance with church observances, running education and social services and dispensing charity. At the national level, it controls a leading daily newspaper, *Ya*, operates its HOAC worker-groups and (before the rise of Opus Dei) supplied ministers to Franco's cabinet. Though it may not see eye to eye with the Falangist components in the régime, Catholic Action forms no sort of opposition movement to the latter but acts rather as a Catholic pressure group which aims at reforming it from within and promoting the christianization of the nation in general. Under the leadership of figures like the late Cardinal Herrera, Bishop of Málaga – a political journalist turned prelate –

it has been particularly concerned with trying to apply to Spain the principles enunciated in successive papal encyclicals. The latter, particularly after the Second Vatican Council, with their new approach to such questions as liturgical reform, the structure of ecclesiastical authority and the attitude of Catholics towards Jews and Protestants, have stirred the Church in Spain to its foundations. With the usual Spanish instinct to go to extremes, some Catholic groups have greeted these reforms in the most radical spirit and demand that a clean sweep be made of all traditional clutter, not only in church affairs but in politics as well. Catholic papers have found themselves in trouble with the authorities for backing workers' and students' demands and some priests have taken part in the activities of the illegal Workers Commissions. The number of worker-priests has risen from a mere handful to ninety in a couple of years. At the other extreme, particularly amongst the older members of the hierarchy, conservative churchmen dig in their heels and see in the slightest concession to change a threat to the cherished traditions of the whole faith and race.

For many Spaniards, however remiss they may be in practising it, Catholicism still remains an essential part of their way of life and of their pride in being Spaniards. This is illustrated by the wide vogue – compounded of piety, patriotism and local loyalties – enjoyed by shrines such as that of Nuestra Señora del Pilar at Saragossa. The story goes that St James, worn out by his missionary labours in Spain, once fell asleep and awoke to see a resplendent vision of the Virgin who promised that the Spaniards would stand as firm as the stone pillar which she left in token on the spot. 'The Virgin's promise has been fulfilled', we read in a popular children's book, 'Spain is, and will always remain, Christian. Neither heretics nor any sort of persecution will be able to overthrow this pillar of our faith. One day the Marxists – bad Spaniards – dropped bombs on this temple with intent to destroy it. But the Virgin miraculously disposed that they should not explode. Here they are in the chapel, bright and shining, exposed to public view, as reminders that the Virgin's love for the Spaniards can do more than all Hell's hatred and that the power of evil must bow before the Queen of Heaven'.[44]

The Virgin of the Pillar is both a national shrine – her feast day falls on 12 October, the day that Columbus discovered America, which is also celebrated as the Day of the Race – and the centre of an intense regional cult.[45] Throughout the length and breadth of Spain one finds a similarly fierce local patriotism, often centring round the patron saint or some relic cherished in the locality. Fervour generally reaches its height at the local fiesta, conducted by the *cofradías* or brotherhoods composed of the saint's devotees, in which the cult object is venerated with the pomp of colourful processions and traditional song and dance. Saints are often esteemed for their reputed efficiency in curing or guarding against specific illness or misfortunes; Santa Lucia for the eyes, San Blas for the throat, Santa Agueda for the breasts, San Roque against pestilence, etc. The devotion lavished upon the fiestas, and particularly on the various facets of the Marian cult – the Virgin of the Pillar, Our Lady of Carmen, of the Rosary, the Immaculate Conception and so on – provides some of the most colourful and moving spectacles in the country. In the remoter parts of Spain piety readily shades off into superstition. In Andalusia, for example, where priests are few, sociologists have observed a 'tremendous lack of any basic religious grounding, probably because this area has been insufficiently christianized. It is an area in which we find the most contradictory religious aspects; whilst great importance is attached to such sacred objects as images, relics, etc. and to offerings (ex-votos, religious habits, tapers, vows, etc.) there is a complete neglect of ordinary religious practices like Sunday mass and frequent Communion. Yet there remains an extraordinary and at times fanatical devotion to patronal saints, certain miracle-working *curandero* saints, miraculous springs, processional cofradías, etc.'[46] When, as now increasingly happens, the devotee turns migrant and goes off to town or factory, he is cut off from his native cult objects and swells the mass of urban workers who live outside any religious influence.

Spain, then, is traditionally and still officially a Catholic country; but how deep in reality does this Catholicism go today? That the Church is beginning to pose the question and sociologists to look for the answer is itself significant. Their findings are sometimes disquieting. An enquiry which the HOAC made in 1957 from a cross-section of more than 15,000 workers showed that nearly 90 per cent described themselves as 'anti-clerical' (most of them adding that they were 'indifferent to religion', and about 41 per cent that they were 'anti-religious'). In the working-class suburbs of Barcelona, only some 2½ per cent of the population attend mass, as compared with between 30–40 per cent in the better-class suburbs of Madrid. In provincial towns and villages, except where, as we have noted, poverty and ecclesiastical neglect go hand in hand, a still higher proportion of the population are practising Catholics. Where religious feeling is particularly strong, the general trend may even be reversed and the workers themselves be drawn into the orbit of the Church. In Vitoria, capital of the Basque province of Álava, though it has become industrialized and doubled its population in the last decade, over 73 per cent of the population, including recent immigrants, are devout practising Catholics. But such cases are exceptional. The general picture is one of a rural and urban proletariat alienated from the Church, whilst Catholicism remains strong amongst the conservative peasantry and the prosperous middle and upper classes. Since it is from the latter that General Franco draws his backing, we are reminded again of the identification between the régime, the propertied classes and the Church.

How long will this picture remain true? If we look at the universities, where discontent with Franco's government has expressed itself in student strikes and demonstrations, we find signs that it may be already beginning to change. For nearly three decades the Church has enjoyed a position of unchallenged influence in university life. Moreover, fewer than three out of every hundred students are the children of agricultural labourers or working-class families; all the rest come from middle- or upper-class backgrounds. Yet it is precisely amongst these students that accepted assumptions and values are being called in question. Opinion polls carried out amongst these reputedly Catholic strongholds have shown surprising results; only 80 per cent of Madrid's university students believe in the existence of God, whilst no more than 61 per cent hold Catholicism to be superior to Protestantism. Only 58 per cent accept papal infallibility in matters of faith, and more than half disapprove of the present close

relations between Church and State in Spain.[47] Is this then the beginning of another swing of the Spanish pendulum from militant
faith to militant incredulity? Liberal Catholics believe that it denotes
less an outright rejection of basic values than a desire to rethink
them in contemporary terms. From this mood of questioning and
probing, of readiness for 'dialogue' with other creeds and ideologies,
they are confident that a new Christian conscience will emerge.

ATTITUDES AND WAYS OF LIFE
Not only in their religious outlook, but in politics and general
attitude to life, the students form that sector of Spanish society which
is most stirred by the winds of change. The demonstrations and
clashes with the police in Madrid, Barcelona, and other university
centres are expressions of the same mood of youthful defiance of
authority which has been a phenomenon common to cities as diverse
as Warsaw, Paris, Tokyo, Rome and New York. Student unrest in
Spain, which led to the closing of several universities during 1967
and 1968 and to the most outspoken protests yet directed against the
Franco régime, has several special features of its own. Students have
been less concerned with specific causes such as Vietnam or better
facilities for study – though feeling on such issues often runs high –
than to vindicate their right to demonstrate per se. Moreover, they often
have the backing of their liberal-minded professors and lecturers,
whose pitifully low salaries are an added economic grievance. Still
more important, the students have been latterly seeking to make
common cause, particularly on such occasions as May Day, with
workers from the growing industrial zones round Madrid and Barcelona. The unofficial but authentic representatives of the student body
are the Sindicatos Democráticos de Estudiantes Españoles, some
two-thirds of whom are probably Christian Democrats and Socialists
who would like to see Spain develop as a parliamentary democracy.
Less than 10 per cent belong to the extreme left, which is itself divided
between adherents of the illegal and pro-Soviet Communist Party,
the Maoists, and the admirers of Che Guevara and Castro. The
government does not make fine distinctions between its enemies, and
the severity with which student dissidence has been repressed has done

much to alienate those middle-class families from which the students predominantly come – families which may be far from sharing their radical views and have hitherto looked with sympathy on a régime claiming to be the bulwark of social order.

The term 'middle-class' may be taken to cover a wide and growing spectrum of Spanish society ranging from the *gente de categoría* – businessmen, rentiers, and senior officials – who have done well for themselves under Franco, to the great majority of modest families who have an uphill struggle to make both ends meet and to keep up the respectable appearance they prize so highly. Though every peseta in the household budget is made to go as far as possible, meanness is never accounted a virtue, for *dignidad* and the reputation of the family call on occasion for open-handed spending. These are the men whom one meets in the streets wearing tie, fresh linen, and dark suits, their wives neatly rather than elegantly dressed, their daughters eschewing mini-skirts and their sons the long hair and informality which is a familiar sight in most western cities. The middle class live in rather drab, overcrowded flats in the tenement-like blocks into which the foreigner seldom goes. There the three-generation family is still common – the head of the family, his wife and children, an in-law or other dependent relative, perhaps a lodger who has recently immigrated to the city from the family's old pueblo. The household may also be completed, though less commonly than before, by a servant. If so, she will be treated as one of the family, since the very name for servant – *criada* – means one who has been brought up with them. To support this household, the breadwinner has normally to take on two or more jobs. The bank-clerk, civil servant, or even university teacher who fights his way onto a bus after a long morning's work – for the Spaniard likes to come home for meals if he can and seldom lunches before two or dines before ten – will emerge after his siesta to begin another job behind bar or counter or as a sports instructor or commission agent. The proverbial indolence of the Spaniard is a myth – or perhaps a pipe-dream. He does not work for the sake of working, but because economic necessity drives him to it. He is no handyman around the house nor devotee of do-it-yourself hobbies; there are women to do the housework and craftsmen to be hired for other needs. Like the hidalgo of old, he would prefer to be relieved of the tiresome necessity of having to earn his living and looks forward to achieving this state some day, either through the receipt of a modest pension or through some stroke of fortune. Hence his addiction to games of chance, *tombola*, and above all, the national lottery. The latter has been established in Spain for more than two centuries, and is patronized by a broader cross-section of the population than are the pools and bingo in Britain. To better his lot and also to rise above the drudgery of pluralism, the Spaniard also looks to a network of personal relationships: his own family connections enlarged by the institution of *compadrazgo* or godfathership, and by the beneficent interventions of an influential patron. He is convinced that the best way to get on in life, whether in business, or for the securing of permits, favours, jobs, and scholarships for his children, and particularly for making his way through the imbroglio of formalities required by the bureaucracy – is to have a suitable *enchufe*, or 'plug-in'. In return, he will render his patron the loyalty and respect which enhances the latter's own importance, and perhaps make some appropriate material return. This is not simply a way of saying that in Spain bribery is rife, but of understanding society as a complex of interlocking solar systems, each revolving around patrons in ascending orders of importance. On the national scale, the centre of the whole system is the Caudillo; on the cosmic scale, God himself, with the apostles, angels, and saints – venerated appropriately as patron saints – the intermediaries for the divine favour.

If Spain is a man's country, woman reigns supreme in Spanish homes. The mother holds the household purse-strings and sets the tone both by virtue of the respect and affection in which she is held, and by her deeply felt and staunchly conservative moral principles. Middle-class children are still usually brought up as devout Catholics, the girls being prepared for the great emotional and social occasion of the First Communion, for which they are decked out in miniature bridal attire. Small boys figure at the same ceremony, preferably clad – apparently without any embarrassment – in the habit of a monk, or (more puzzlingly) in the regalia of a full admiral.

Nowhere is the changing pattern of Spanish society more marked than in the new role and status which women are beginning to enjoy. The country has never lacked women of character and ability. One has only to think of Queen Isabel and Saint Teresa in the days of Spain's greatness; nor, in all the talk about Spain's ensuing decline, has anyone had the temerity to suggest that it was the women who were degenerate. On the contrary, the firm character, natural intelli-gence and physical energy, as well as the grace and beauty of Spanish women, have often been extolled. Yet undoubtedly they were generally kept in ignorance and social inferiority. Perhaps the Mos-lem tradition of seclusion died hard, or they may simply have pre-ferred the reality of matriarchal authority within the home to the formalities of social emancipation. At all events, they had to wait for the Republic before they received the vote, and for the Civil War for the grim privilege of equality of suffering and heroism beside their menfolk. That ordeal saw the emergence of notable women on each side; La Pasionaria, the famous Communist leader, and for the Falange, Pilar Primo de Rivera, sister of its founder and now head of the remarkable Servicio Social, in which every woman has to spend six months in some form of training and service to the community.

Spanish society traditionally recognized only two roles for women: either marriage or the religious life. Even now it can hardly take the idea seriously that a woman may wish to remain unmarried and dedicate herself to a career. 'Spanish society today still regards spin-sters as something exceptional', we are assured, 'women who are certainly abnormal, and often pathological cases'.[48] But economic pressures are steadily forcing more and more women to find work outside the home. Until 1950, women made up a mere 7 per cent of the nation's labour force; in a decade and a half the proportion has risen to more than 17 per cent – a figure still low compared with Italy's 25 per cent and the United Kingdom's 31 per cent. Legally, women suffer few discriminations in finding employment, and they are theoretically entitled to the same pay as men. In practice, three-quarters of them are confined to the most menial, mechanical and poorly paid work. In theory, they enjoy equal educational oppor-tunities and there are as many girls as boys in the elementary schools.

But far fewer go on to secondary education and in the universities only one-quarter or one-fifth of the students are women. It is consequently still rare to find women in the professions. There are only three women delegates to the national Cortes and the same number holding university chairs. The government lays great stress on the importance of maintaining the sanctity of family life and fears that this may be endangered or neglected if a mother seeks a second career outside it. A wife is consequently required by law to obtain her husband's formal permission before taking on a job. Since every married man is entitled, after the birth of a second child, to receive a marriage allowance which he forfeits if his wife goes out to work, it is not surprising that this consent is often withheld. So the Spanish woman stands today on the threshold of a wider world, no longer compelled, as the proverb expects of a virtuous woman, 'to keep to her home with a broken leg', yet still not quite able or willing to seize the new opportunities which are within her reach.

Yet in many respects the traditional mode of life and scale of values have proved quite flexible enough to absorb the impact of new economic forces and modern communications media which might have been thought injurious to women. Cinema-going, for instance, once looked upon as a grave threat to morality, is now an established habit regulated not only by the official classification of films on lines similar to those of our X, A and U certificates, but also by a more detailed and stringent grading drawn up by the semi-official Heads of Families Association, whose warnings of 'Gravely Dangerous' and milder admonitions are published in the press and taken to heart by Catholic families. Spain has now also passed the threshold of the television age, though the habit is neither so widespread as with us nor its effects similar. The Spaniard values conversation too highly to surrender this pleasure in order to sit for hours with his family in front of the television set. It is usual to find television in cafés or restaurants, where it appears to absorb the attention of waiters and reinforces that background of noise without which enjoyment of life seems not to be complete. Whether it will end by weakening the attraction of the *tertulia* – the informal gathering of friends round a favourite café table – remains to be seen.

The most famous of all Spanish institutions – bull-fighting – still retains its popularity, though there are those who claim that the bulls are not so fierce nor the toreadors so skilful and intrepid as in their youth. Certainly, the most famous of contemporary bull-fighters, El Cordobés, has recently suffered the indignity of being booed in his home town and was once humiliated by a spectator jumping into the ring, seizing the beast by the horns, and waltzing around with it to show that it was more of a lamb than a bull. Many Spaniards never go near a bull-ring, either because – as became fashionable in liberal and left-wing circles some decades ago – they disapprove of bull-fighting in principle or because they are indifferent to it, or because they keep their enthusiasm for Real Madrid or some other star team. It cannot be said that football has driven out bull-fighting; the Spaniard's mode of life, in this as in other matters, has proved elastic enough to allow him to assimilate the one without rejecting the other. It has been sometimes asserted – and by their own moralists – that the Spaniards' besetting sin is envy. If this is so, it seems to operate on the personal but not on a national level. A Spaniard may covet a sleek American limousine and his wife be fascinated by the lure of a modern kitchen, but for all this they are not tempted to become converts to the American, or to any other, way of life.

CONTEMPORARY LITERATURE

If Spain can boast the achievement of a certain degree of material progress in the last three decades, nothing comparable can be claimed in the fields of culture and literature. The prevailing mediocrity has two main causes: first, the loss of almost all her outstanding writers and intellectuals after the Civil War, and secondly, the climate of censorship and conformity in which those who remain in Spain still have to work. Some writers perished as a direct result of the war: García Lorca before a firing squad and Miguel Hernández, the communist peasant poet, in an Alicante jail. Many found new homes in American universities or the Spanish-speaking republics of Latin America. Perhaps painters, musicians and scholars suffer less than writers from exile. Picasso, Miró and Salvador Dali are in any case great cosmopolitan figures and Casals' stature as a musician,

Buñuel's as a film director, or that of Américo Castro and Sánchez Albornoz as scholars can scarcely be said to have been diminished by exile. But to be cut off from his natural environment is a profound misfortune for a writer. He can seldom put down new roots deep enough to give his genius the full nourishment it needs. It is thus not surprising that exiled novelists like Ramón J. Sender and Max Aub remain obsessively concerned with the traumatic experience of the Civil War, nor that the Spanish government should choose to keep their books out of the country. Lately, Madrid has somewhat relaxed its restrictions and the Spanish public is now at last able to read – a quarter of a century after its first publication – Sender's monumental *Crónica del Alba*. Spanish novelists living in Spain, like Angel María de Lera in his *Las Últimas Banderas*, are also now publishing work treating the Civil War with an objectivity and compassion very different from the treatment hitherto prescribed by the régime. Contemporary social problems are also beginning to be treated with a more sympathetic insight, as in Caballero Bonald's *Dos Días de Setiembre*, an account of two days in the life of agricultural labourers during the grape harvest.

Most, however, of the fiction which has poured from the presses in recent years has been frankly escapist. Honourable exceptions to this trend have been a number of sound, prize-winning novels, and the work of two robust writers working in Spain's picaresque tradition and in that of the pessimistic realism of Pío Baroja (whose vast output continued to within a short time of his death in 1956); Camilo José Cela (b. 1916) and Juan Goytisolo (b. 1931). In *La Familia de Pascual Duarte* Cela tells the life-story of a rootless labourer whose brutal and senseless crimes lead him at length to the gallows. There followed *La Colmena*, depicting the swarming, seamy life of Madrid, and a number of unconventional books of travel to little known and primitive parts of Spain. Cela's vision of his country is bleak and black, perhaps a little too aggressively intended to shock – '*tremendismo*' is a term which has been applied to it – but vigorous and unflinchingly honest. Goytisolo, who has also written accounts of his travels in the grim, poverty-stricken corners of Spain, writes about the futility and corruption of bourgeois society (*Fiesta*), youth driven to criminal violence or political extremism (*Duelo en el Paraíso*), children brutalized by the inhumanity of war. This is strong meat for a régime which likes to take credit for Spain's economic miracle and the re-establishment of Christian values, and Goytisolo has had to publish his latest novel, *Señas de Identidad*, abroad.

The foremost poets of their generation – Juan Ramón Jiménez, Antonio Machado, Rafael Alberti, Jorge Guillén – were lost to Spain in the cultural diaspora. Machado did not survive the flight into France; Jiménez lived on for nearly twenty years in exile. With the death of this Nobel prize-winner and author of many volumes of exquisite verse, Spain lost her last poet of incontestably the first rank, though there are a number of younger poets – mostly Andalusians – publishing distinguished work in Spain today. Nor is there any dearth of young playwrights, though none has yet shown signs of stepping into the shoes of that other Nobel prize-winner, Jacinto Benavente (1866–1954). Those who wish to forsake light comedy and conventional romance for plays which deal with serious controversial issues risk having their work banned. Thus Alfonso Sastre, one of the most talented of the younger dramatists, has not yet been able to stage his play dealing with the life and execution for heresy of the sixteenth-century Spaniard Miguel Servet, famous for his pioneering work in the circulation of the blood. That Spain is still a far from safe place for writers of unorthodox views is shown by the preposterous misadventure of Fernando Arrabal, a Spanish playwright living in Paris who returned on a visit to Spain in 1967. The authorities took exception to a dedication which he had written in one of his books and had him arrested for the use of terms deemed offensive to God and the *patria*. He only escaped imprisonment by assuring the court that the offending passage referred not to the patria but to his cat Patra (short for 'Cleopatra'), and not to God, but to the god Pan – a dénouement surely as bizarre as anything one meets with in his own Theatre of the Absurd.

The author of an offending play, book or article does not generally escape so lightly. Courts still hand out fines, confiscation orders and prison sentences. Recent cases include six months' imprisonment for a poet and two years for a journalist for the publication of a poem deemed offensive to the armed forces, twelve years, *in absentia*, for the author of a couple of anti-Franco articles published in a French magazine, and the prosecution of Alfonso Comín, author of a scholarly work on the sociology of southern Spain, for contributing an article to a progressive French Catholic journal. Even the classics may fall foul of the censor; the plays of Valle Inclán, for instance, have been heavily expurgated and sometimes banned. This repressive climate in which Spanish writers have to work contrasts with the greater toleration now accorded to the work of foreign authors. An astonishingly wide range of translations, including books by known Marxists, are on sale in Spanish bookshops, and theatregoers can now see plays by such writers as Sartre and Brecht. Currents of thought, which still may not be propagated by indigenous writers, seep in from abroad. To be completely isolated from Europe, either intellectually or politically, is no longer thought feasible or desirable. As we shall see in the next chapter, Spain's relationship with the outside world has been changing.

21 This deserted pueblo shows how the flight from the land by the younger generation in search of jobs and better living conditions is leading to serious rural depopulation in some provinces. 22 Madrid, the capital and geographical centre of Spain, attracts many of these emigrants. It has been growing fast, and now has a population of three million.

23 Olives and vines account for an important part of Spain's agricultural production.

24 Toledo was an important city long before Madrid was built. It was famous for its fine sword-blades (still manufactured there) and its impregnable position overlooking the Tagus. The siege of its Alcázar, now rebuilt, was an epic chapter in the Civil War. Its ancient churches, museums and many paintings by El Greco draw thousands of visitors.

25 Catalonia's most famous monastery is perched high up on Montserrat, a mountain of fantastic shape. Here St Ignatius held all-night vigil in front of the venerated image of the Virgin before devoting himself to founding the Jesuit Order.

26   Cartagena, in the south-east of Spain, has one of the country's largest oil refineries. There is little about this up-to-date naval base and maritime centre to recall its ancient Carthaginian origin except its name.

27   Bilbao, the capital of the Basque province of Biscay, is the chief port of northern Spain and the most important centre of heavy industry.

28 Copper being processed
in a mill outside Cordova.
Spain has been noted from
the earliest times as a producer
of metals.

29 The new dam at Pataño
de Aldeadávila.
The programme of dam
construction for purposes of
irrigation and hydro-electric
power is an important factor
for the modernization of the
Spanish economy.

30 Religious processions are still a frequent spectacle in Spain. Here an image of Our Lady, surrounded by wax candles and accompanied by hooded, black-robed penitents, is borne through the streets of Cordova.
31 Dancing to the sound of the guitar is not just something put on for the benefit of foreign tourists. It is still the spontaneous expression of the gaiety and exuberance of popular life, particularly in the southern and eastern provinces of Spain.
32 The mule still remains the traditional beast of burden, even in the prosperous and efficient sherry industry. 33 The austere plains of La Mancha, with their flocks of sheep and their windmills, have changed little since the days when Don Quixote rode across them in quest of adventure.

34 Gaudí's highly original churches and houses, with their air of melting stone-work, are a distinctive feature of the Catalan capital. 35 This new technical college at Alcolea, in southern Spain, has been built to help produce the many technicians and skilled workers which the country needs for its expanding economy. The open-air theatre in the foreground is a reminder of the Spaniards' passion for the stage.

7   Spain and the world

SPAIN HAS TRADITIONALLY found outlets for her national energies in three directions; North Africa, Europe and America. These areas are still the main fields for her political and commercial interests today.

We have already noted the enormously important part that Africa has played throughout Spanish history. Not only has it served as a spring-board for successive invasions of the Iberian peninsula, but it has in turn been regarded as the natural zone for Spanish expansion. When Spain ceased to be a European power and lost the remnants of her empire in the New World, she still clung tenaciously to her foot-hold in Africa. Thanks to Ceuta and Melilla and the smaller garri-son towns, or *plazas de soberanía*, which had long been in her posses-sion, Spain secured for herself some of the pickings when Morocco was dismembered by the great powers before the First World War. France seized the lion's share, but Spain gained the coastal zone round Tangier (excluding the city itself) and a tract of desert territory south of the vast French Protectorate. Although this Southern Protectorate had to be abandoned after Spain had recognized Moroccan inde-pendence in 1955, her stake in Africa remained substantial. In addition to the plazas de soberanía, she possesses Ifni, a rectangle of territory fifteen by forty miles in area on the Moroccan coast, the Spanish Sahara, with its small settlements and larger nomad popula-tion to the north of Mauritania, and still further south, Spanish Guinea, comprising Río Muni and the island of Fernando Po. Following a referendum held on 11 August 1968 Spain announced that Spanish Guinea would be granted independence within two months. It seems, however, that 'far from being prepared to walk off the stage, she is determined to create a Hispano-Guinean state which will bear witness to Spanish language and culture in Black Africa'.[49]

These African possessions, scattered though they are and hitherto of little significance in themselves, have had an important influence on Metropolitan Spain. They still represent a token empire, a field where Spaniards continue to act out their imperial role and from which they may return, when the hour of destiny strikes, to play a decisive part in the affairs of the mother country. Under the fierce African sun, the officer corps acquired a distinctive mentality and ethos, a nationalistic and professional pride intolerant of the squabbling politicians at home. From 1921-6, Spanish rule was challenged by the revolt of the Riff tribesmen under their formidable leader Abd-el-Krim, and a Spanish Army was cut to pieces in the disaster of Anual. This humiliation showed up the feebleness of the monarchy and led to the establishment of the dictatorship of Primo de Rivera, who crushed the rebels and re-established the Spanish army's power-base in Africa from which, ten years later, Franco launched his assault on the Republic at the head of Spanish-led Moorish troops.

Franco's victory opened up still more dazzling prospects. Would not the Axis armies then sweeping to victory in Europe enable Spain to rebuild an empire for herself in Africa? As the price of Spanish intervention on the side of Hitler and Mussolini, Franco demanded the reversion of Gibraltar, all French Morocco, part of Algeria and extensions to the existing Spanish holdings on the west coast of Africa. Spain's demands were pitched too high; there was Vichy France to be conciliated and Germany's own African ambitions to be satisfied. The vision of a Spanish empire in Africa faded as Axis fortunes declined. By the time the Allies landed in North Africa in November 1942, the global balance of power had shifted sufficiently to discourage Franco from ordering his 150,000 troops stationed there to move against them. Since then, Spain has been less concerned with expanding her African possessions than with safeguarding those she already has. She has to be on her guard against both the expansionist vigour of Arab nationalism and the subversive contagion of 'Arab socialism'.

Spain's historical and current ties with the Continent are sometimes invoked to justify her playing an alleged role as 'the bridge to Islam'. Since she was herself for so long under Moorish influence, the Arab states of today are supposed to feel a special affinity towards her which Madrid does its best to foster by such gestures as refusing to recognize the state of Israel. But the 'bridge to Islam' seems a flimsy structure. At times of tension between the Arab states and the West – as in the Arab–Israeli war of 1967 – it has not enabled Spain to play any effective intermediary role. Moreover, her own troubles with the Arab world, especially now that Soviet influence there is on the increase, seem likely to mount. Morocco has made no secret of her designs on Ifni; it was invaded in 1957 by an unofficial 'Army of Liberation' and the dispute was only settled after Spain had agreed to relinquish her Southern Protectorate. But this concession has by no means satisfied Rabat's ambitions and in 1967 Spain was obliged to open negotiations for the transfer of Ifni to Morocco. The discovery in the Spanish Sahara of what promises to be the world's richest phosphate deposits, which Spain hopes to exploit with the help of American capital, has sharpened rivalries in that area. Moroccan irredentist agitation in the spring of 1967 prompted a visit to the Spanish Sahara by Spain's Minister of War, who reaffirmed his country's right to that territory and her determination to protect its population against unspecified 'jackals'. Then there is the future of Melilla, today a preponderantly European city which has been in continuous Spanish possession for nearly 500 years, and Ceuta, once valued as a potential alternative and challenge to Gibraltar. It is commonly believed that a tacit understanding exists that Morocco should not press her claims against these enclaves until Spain receives satisfaction for her own claims on Gibraltar. Whatever the future holds, it seems unlikely to offer Spain much scope for advance in Africa. The pendulum seems to be swinging unmistakably towards Europe.

General Franco's Spain came to birth in the Europe of Hitler and Mussolini; her problem has since been to find a secure and honourable place in the Europe of the victorious democracies. Italy and Germany made themselves acceptable by repudiating their Fascist and

Nazi past. But Spain is still governed by an ageing Caudillo and a 'movement' which, for all their recent show of liberalization, have never renounced their anti-democratic origins. That a régime so distastefully anachronistic in the eyes of most West Europeans should not only have survived but have been visibly moving towards full acceptance by contemporary Europe is a tribute to the astuteness of her leader. His admirers claim still more for him: it is not Spain, they assert, that has altered course, but the democracies, aware at last of the Bolshevik peril and the need to close ranks against the Soviet Union which the Caudillo foresaw from the outset, that have come round to his position. The development of the Cold War, in short, vindicated – in the phrase of one of his apologists – that Spain was Right.[50]

Even before the end of the Civil War, Franco had signified Spain's alignment with the Axis powers by adding his signature to those of Germany, Italy and Japan in the Anti-Comintern Pact. The following November, he concluded a pact of friendship with Germany, which was supplemented by secret undertakings to allow her the use of naval facilities in Spanish ports and a 'cooperative' role in connection with Franco's police, press and propaganda.[51] In October 1940, the Fuehrer and the Caudillo met at Hendaye on the French frontier to discuss proposals for further war-time cooperation, including a German plan for a combined operation against Gibraltar. Allied fortunes were then at their nadir, and Britain stood alone against the Axis. Spain seemed to be on the brink of joining the side which must inevitably win. Why, then, did not Franco give the fateful word? Not out of any coolness for the Axis cause, for his sympathies are a matter of record.[52] Perhaps the pact then in force between Hitler and Stalin was not altogether to his liking; certainly he had misgivings about the capacity of his still devastated country to wage even a short war, and about the loyalties of a still bitterly divided people. Moreover, Spain desperately needed the food, petroleum and other vital products which she could only obtain with the goodwill of the Allies. More important still, the Germans would not pledge themselves to pay the full price which Franco demanded in return for full Spanish participation in the war: not only the reversion of Gibraltar but the acquisition of a new empire in Africa. When

Hitler launched his attack on the Soviet Union, Franco did indeed intervene militarily to repay his 'blood-debt' to the extent of despatching some 14,000 volunteers of the 'Blue Division' to fight with the Germans on the Eastern Front. But the entry of the United States into the war redressed the balance of global forces in favour of the Allies and reinforced the case for prudence. Franco continued to give the Axis powers every aid he could short of actually joining in the war on their side.

By the autumn of 1944, it began to look certain that the Axis would not, after all, win the war, and Franco made a sudden bid for reinsurance with the Allies. In a letter to Churchill, who had stated in the Commons a few months before that he looked forward to 'increasingly good relations and an extremely fertile trade between Spain and this country', the Caudillo proposed that Britain and Spain should join forces in helping to protect Western Europe against 'the insidious power of Bolshevism'. This, and other last-minute overtures to the Allies, were rejected, and the Franco régime found itself cold-shouldered by the post-war world as a Fascist pariah and excluded from the United Nations and the Marshall Plan. France, Britain and the United States even affirmed in a tripartite declaration of March 1946 that the Spanish people could not expect a 'full and cordial association' with them whilst Franco remained in control of their affairs. Except for Portugal, with whose like-minded dictator Franco had concluded a non-aggression treaty in 1939 and the Iberian Pact of 1943, Spain was ostracized by all the countries of Europe. France, remembering the support given by the Caudillo to the Vichy Government, showed herself particularly hostile. For two years after the end of the world war, the frontier between France and Spain remained closed, and Spanish republican exiles, with the assistance of French *maquisards*, used French territory as a base for raids over the Pyrenees. Franco bided his time and was able to repay France in her own coin by favouring the Algerian rebels ten years later. Nevertheless long before that time it had become clear that the policy of ostracism had failed and the western powers – particularly the United States – were moving towards a remarkable volte-face in their attitude towards the Franco régime.

The most important factor in this change of attitude towards Spain was the onset of the Cold War. How this was to cause a reversal in United States policy and lead to the conclusion of the 1953 bases agreement we shall see shortly. To some extent, the Cold War was also instrumental in softening French hostility to Spain and it was a sign of the milder climate when Spain was admitted, along with fifteen other countries, to the United Nations in 1955. After General de Gaulle's return to power in 1958, the rapprochement between France and Spain gathered impetus. French and Spanish policies in Africa, hitherto in conflict, were reconciled and De Gaulle declared that he favoured the inclusion of Spain in NATO. Even more important, France let it be known that she would support a Spanish application to join the Common Market. But France's partners, both in NATO and in EEC, received these proposals coolly. When, in February 1962, Spain made her first application to begin negotiations with the Common Market countries, Italy opposed her admission on economic grounds, for Spanish agricultural products would be in competition with her own. Belgium and the Netherlands rejected Spain on political grounds. On renewing the application in 1964, Spain was offered a commercial treaty affecting industrial goods, with the promise to review, after a couple of years, the possibility of granting her associated status. In 1967, when negotiations were re-opened, the EEC held out the prospect of a six-year period of association, but gave no firm pledge that this would lead on to full membership.

What would Spain stand to gain by ultimate membership of the European Economic Community? It would, of course, mark the end of the long period of ostracism and set the seal on her full political acceptability. The economic consequences would be far-reaching. The EEC already accounts for more than one-third of Spain's foreign trade. Of recent years, her exports to member countries have been falling whilst her imports have mounted, so that she has consequently accumulated a serious adverse balance of trade. The disparity is likely to intensify the longer she remains outside the Common Market. But should she gain admission, important sectors of her economy will be correspondingly stimulated. Tourism, and certain branches of agricultural production (grapes, citrus fruit, olives, etc.) could expect rapid expansion. On her industry, much of which has grown up behind high tariffs and is handicapped by inadequate investment and high production costs, the effect is likely, at least initially, to be more dubious. Certain sectors, such as her flourishing shipyards, could probably do well, but her iron and steel industry, which operates at costs substantially higher than European levels and with a productivity 50 per cent less, would be hard put to it to make good. One enquiry into the results to be expected from Spain's participation in EEC has reached the significant conclusion that the beneficial effects would be strongest precisely in those areas of Spain – the south and south-east – which have hitherto been most neglected economically.[53] Association with Europe would thus offer – according to this forecast – 'the possibility of being an instrument to correct the regional disequilibrium of Spain'. But would association in itself have this effect? Only if – other economists argue – the government introduces a preliminary or concurrent programme of radical structural reforms, particularly agrarian and fiscal reform, which would iron out the immense disparities between rich and poor, increase the purchasing power of the underprivileged masses and place the national economy on a generally healthier basis. Without such changes, it is argued, Spain would inevitably sink to the bottom in a growing polarization between the economically strong and the economically weak counries. What advantage would she gain from joining the European family, if she were only to remain its poor relation?[54]

So the pros and cons of joining the Common Market, and the chances of being permitted to do so, continue to be as hotly debated as they are in Britain, Spain's fellow applicant for admission and important trading partner. In the last century, Britain made considerable investments in Spain and still has an important economic stake (the Río Tinto mines, the wine industry, etc.) in the country. Of recent years she has been increasing her investments, though they are now vastly overshadowed by those of the United States, and she now ranks fourth – after that country, the EEC and Switzerland – as a source of investment. Britain also holds fourth place (after the United States, W. Germany, and France) as a market for Spanish exports and as a source for her imports. Trade between the two countries remains brisk and British tourists continue to flock to Spain in their hundreds of thousands, although Britain has not gone so far or so fast as some other states in revising her originally unfavourable view of the Franco régime. Labour governments, in particular, have continued to maintain towards her an attitude of reserve. In 1951, objections were raised in London to associating Spain with the defence of the West, and in 1964 Britain called off participation in the annual joint naval manœuvres with Spain, which prompted Madrid to cancel the projected construction of frigates under British licence and with British technical assistance. Spain, on her side, nurses a grievance against Britain that she has been voicing with increasing insistence in recent years – the question of Gibraltar.

The return of Gibraltar, which has been in British hands since its capture in 1704, has long been an aim of Spanish policy. Madrid is now pressing strongly for a revision of Article 10 of the Treaty of Utrecht, which gives Britain sovereignty over the 'Town and Castle of Gibraltar, together with the fortifications and forts thereunto belonging', and denounces Britain for illegally creating a 'second Gibraltar' in the neutral zone between the Rock and the Spanish mainland, where the airstrip, vital for defence, communications and the development of the tourist trade, has been constructed. She also argues that the present status of Gibraltar is a survival of outmoded colonialism, that the Gibraltarians are an artificially created and transient population and that the Rock has, in any event, lost much of its value as a military and naval base. Britain is also accused of conniving at large-scale smuggling by means of the six thousand Spanish workers who stream in and out of the colony for their daily employment.

Since 1966, the Spanish Government has been stepping up its campaign for the return of Gibraltar by canvassing world support for its case, chiefly at the United Nations, and by bringing increasing pressure to bear against the British authorities and the inhabitants of the Rock – the harassing of vehicular traffic wishing to enter Spain, refusal to permit the two thousand Spanish women normally employed there to enter Gibraltar (with hints that similar action will

be taken with regard to male labour as soon as alternative employment can be found for them in Spain), the introduction of measures
'to protect Spanish air-space' (and thus strangle the colony's air
traffic) and similar moves against its sea-borne traffic by moving Spanish warships into waters hitherto treated as British. Britain has refused
to yield on the issue of sovereignty, but has suggested that the dispute
should be referred to the International Court and has offered Spain
representation and other rights in the colony and a revision of its
constitution, whilst stepping up material assistance to Gibraltar to
counteract the effect of the restrictions imposed by Spain. In Sep-
tember 1967 a Referendum was held in which the Gibraltarians were
offered the choice of reversion to Spain or retaining their link with
Britain. Ninety-nine per cent declared themselves in favour of Britain
and only 44 votes were cast for Spain. In the United Nations,
however – both in the Committee of Twenty-Four and in the General
Assembly – Spain has rallied a good deal of support for her claims
and she argues that the Gibraltarians' vote should be discounted
since it violates a United Nations recommendation that the problem
should be settled by direct talks between Britain and Spain. To
strengthen her hand still further, she has made it clear to the United
States (which abstained in the United Nations voting) that she
considered the question of Gibraltar to be linked to an issue of direct
concern to Washington – the future of American bases in Spain.

The key-stone of Spanish-American relations is the 1953 Pact
of Madrid. The three inter-related agreements comprising this Pact –
the Defence Agreement specifically concerned with the bases, a
Mutual Defence Assistance Agreement providing American loans,
equipment and training facilities for the Spanish armed forces, and
an Economic Aid Agreement – marked a turning point in Spain's
foreign relations. They signified the end of Spain's international
isolation and her acceptance as a partner, if not as a fully fledged ally,
of the greatest power of the western world. The reversal of the United
States' policy of ostracizing Spain was due to the Pentagon's need of
Spanish harbours and additional air bases in the intensification of the
Cold War and the American military involvement in Korea. Franco,
for his part, welcomed the new status of international respectability

and the prospect of economic assistance resulting from the agree-ments. The new Spanish-American relationship was conceived as a partnership; the bases, though financed and built by the United States, were not to be ceded or merely leased, but held jointly. They comprised the great naval air base of Rota in the bay of Cadiz (to serve the needs of the Sixth Fleet and, subsequently, to accommodate Polaris submarines), air bases outside Madrid, Seville and (since discontinued) Saragossa, together with a number of lesser bases, supply depots and radar installations and an oil pipe running from Rota to Saragossa to link the major bases. The initial agreement was for ten years. It was renewed in 1963 on terms which brought Spain still closer to the status of a full ally of the United States and came up again for further renewal in 1968.

Now that the agreements have been in effect for a decade and a half, we can make some assessment of their impact. The Spanish armed forces have certainly benefited greatly from United States technology, equipment and training. The Army, now some two hundred thou-sand men strong, is a more modern, professionally competent fighting force than before. The national economy has been stimulated by the Economic Aid Agreement and American capital invest-ment, which rose from $6 million in 1961 to over $44 million in 1965, is a crucial factor in the country's economic expansion. The value of the bases themselves has probably declined in strategic terms, following the development of the inter-continental ballistic missiles, and the Spanish cities in whose vicinity the bases were built now come within the range of Soviet nuclear retaliation. The loss of four hydrogen bombs after a mid-air collision over Palomares in southern Spain in 1966, which involved the United States in heavy compensation for damage to property and contamination of crops, provoked alarm and resentment and also brought home the perils as well as the advantages of the American alliance. The restric-tions announced at the beginning of 1968 by President Johnson on the future rate of American investment abroad and other measures in defence of the dollar showed also how dependent the Spanish economy had become on American resources. The alliance itself has never been to the liking of all Spaniards. The stationing of foreign troops on Spanish soil has been a hard pill for nationalist opinion to swallow; furthermore, General de Gaulle's coolness towards NATO has strengthened the feeling in some quarters that disengagement from Washington's embrace would be more consonant with Spanish dignity and interests. The extreme Left is uneasy to see Spain ranged in the Western camp, ultra-conservatives have denounced the agreements as 'opening the door to heresy', whilst anti-Franco Spaniards blame the United States for propping up a dictatorial régime. The Spanish Government itself is showing signs that its anti-communist bark, which served it so well when the Cold War was at its sharpest, is worse than its bite. It has established consular and commercial relations with one Communist state – Roumania – and has diplomatic relations and a lively trade with another – Cuba. There has even been talk of Madrid's recognizing the Soviet Union, with whom Spain already has a maritime agreement and expanding trade links.[55] Though a resumption of full relations with Moscow can hardly be expected in Franco's life-time, since American good-will continues to be essential to the economic, military and political health of the government, Madrid will no doubt seek to exploit her more benign attitude towards the communist powers to exact a higher price from Washington, in terms of economic support and political backing for her Gibraltar claims, in return for the continued use of facilities which are still of great value to the United States as staging-posts for aerial refuelling, for their early-warning radar system, and as a base for her Polaris submarines.

If Spain is now linked to the United States by mutual interest, she feels bound by deep-rooted sentiment to that other America – the Spanish-speaking half of the continent which she discovered, conquered, colonized and ruled for three centuries. Invoking the slogan of *Hispanidad*, Madrid has been striving to turn to solid economic and political account the 'special relationship' declared to stem from the common racial, cultural and historical roots shared by Spain and her ex-colonies. Politically, this drive has yielded some dividends in the form of support from the Latin American delegates to the United Nations for Spain's claims on Gibraltar. Economically, it has resulted in an increase of trade, though Latin America still accounts for only a modest proportion of her total foreign trade (17 per cent in 1966). Spain's imports from Latin America increased from $67 million in 1960 to $259 million in 1965, and her exports from $57 to $122 million. The problem has been to narrow this unfavourable trade gap, for Spain bought from Latin America during that period about twice as much as she sold to it. In 1965, the Spanish government announced that it would extend 1,000 million dollars worth of credit over a ten-year period and followed up this offer by sending trade missions to negotiate bilateral agreements with individual countries. By the end of 1966 Spanish imports from Latin America had risen to $326 million and her exports to $216 million – more than two-thirds of her imports. Some advocates of Hispanidad dream that Spain will one day join a Hispano-American Common Market and serve as a sort of 'bridge to Europe'. These hopes are chimerical, for the Latin American countries wish to develop their own powerful economic links with the United States and directly with Europe. Nevertheless, it is true that the agricultural policies of the EEC countries are a matter of growing concern to them, and many Latin American business men are looking towards Spain as an increasingly attractive market.

A remarkable feature of the Spanish trade drive in Latin America is that it has even extended to Cuba. From an annual average of $30 million in the years preceding Castro's rise to power, Spanish-Cuban trade increased to $97 million in 1964. Spain buys Cuban sugar and tobacco and sells wine, agricultural equipment, lorries and the ships which have enabled Castro to build up a large new merchant fleet. This is the more remarkable in that the large and prosperous Spanish community living in Cuba was dealt a crushing blow when Castro expropriated all foreign-owned enterprises and subsequently arranged for the repatriation of more than fifteen thousand Spanish citizens. There have been delicate diplomatic incidents, such as when the Spanish Ambassador rushed to a Havana television studio to interrupt Castro in the midst of a tirade he deemed insulting to Spanish honour. There is also the fact that anti-Franco refugees have been given ample facilities to organize and conduct their propaganda in Cuba. Nevertheless, correct diplomatic and flourishing trade relations subsist between this communist outpost and Franco's anti-Bolshevik bastion in Europe. Cuban defiance of the United States strikes a responsive chord in Spanish hearts. When, in 1964, Cuban exiles, acting with suspected connivance of the United States, attacked a Spanish merchant ship bound for Cuba, a wave of anti-American indignation swept Spain. At such times, blood proves thicker than ideology and the Spanish press has ruefully admitted 'the admiration felt in many social sectors for the régime of Fidel Castro. Spain's intransigent stand against communism almost seems to break down when it comes to Cuba. We can only explain it by the affection they have for a nation far removed in distance but very close in Spanish sentiment.'

Modest as is the place which Spain must take today beside the more industrially developed countries of Europe and beneath the shadow of the two super-powers, the special contribution which she has made to the formation of the Spanish-speaking nations overseas adds a new extension to her national personality. It is not – as the Falangists dreamed – that she will ever recover her old imperial predominance amongst the twenty republics of Latin America. But to each of them she has given in varying degrees (if we except Portuguese-speaking Brazil and French-speaking Haiti) something of her own essence. It was natural for the conquistadors to christen the empire they wrested from Montezuma 'New Spain'. Nor can we fail to note today the indelible imprint which Spain has left on the lush shores of the Caribbean, the great cities and lonely pampas of the mainland, even in the remotest Andean valleys. No portrait of Spain would be complete without some awareness of this extra dimension, this American incarnation of her true genius; for – to paraphrase Kipling's line – what should they know of Spain who only Spain know? Spain only became fully herself in rising to the stupendous challenge of discovering, subduing, colonizing and administering the vast and distant lands of the New World. And if the task finished by exhausting her, she can console herself with the thought that her children, even when disowning her, are still often more Spanish in their essence than they know, and that if she has lost them as off-spring she is now learning to live with them as sister-nations.

North Africa, Europe, and America – these are the parts of the world with which Spain's future will be most closely bound up. But the world itself is changing, and the way in which it changes must vitally affect the nature of post-Franco Spain. A France which repudiates Gaullism and swings to the Left would improve the prospects of the Left inside Spain too. An Africa swept by fresh tides of nationalism would endanger her possessions south of the Straits. A President of the United States pledged to cut down American commitments overseas would entail a revision of Spain's whole military and economic position. And if Spain wishes to find a model for some new line of political development, might she not turn her gaze to one or other of the experiments now taking place in Spanish America – Castro's brand of Cuban-style Communism, the Christian Democrats' 'revolution in liberty' in Chile, or the Mexican recipe for democracy and economic development through a virtually one-party state?

These are all influences which may help to determine Spain's new place in the world. But the decisive factor will be the forces which have been steadily gathering inside Spain herself, beneath the crust of General Franco's thirty-year-old régime. Change must come, though it will not necessarily be violent or even particularly rapid. There is little to indicate, as in the tense years of the early 'thirties, a pre-revolutionary situation; certainly the Spanish Communist Party seems to be working on the assumption that no such situation at present exists. Spain will probably develop as a republic or some form of monarchy. The Carlist minority still hopes for an old-style royal autocracy which will restore the glories of sixteenth-century Spain. Others would prefer to see Don Juan Carlos on the throne, with many of the features of the present régime continuing under his pliant rule. The liberal-minded set their hopes on his father, Don Juan, whom they believe to have the makings of a democratic and constitutional monarch. In the meantime, the ageing but still all-powerful Caudillo keeps his own counsel and leaves his people to the solace of the old Spanish proverb – 'Patience – and shuffle the cards!'

Notes on the text

I THE LAND AND THE PEOPLE

1 Pitt Rivers relates one such case, which occurred at the *pueblo* of Gastor at the end of the last century, in his interesting book, *The People of the Sierra*, London, 1954, pp 17–18.
2 V. S. Pritchett: *The Spanish Temper*, London, 1954, p 15.
3 This problem has been investigated by Francisco Candel in a book which created a considerable stir, *Los Otros Catalanes*, Madrid, 1965.

2 CROSS AND CRESCENT

4 Vernet, Juan, *Los Musulmanes Españoles*, Barcelona, 1961, pp 12–13.
5 Hole, E., *Andalus: Spain under the Muslims*, London, 1958, p 34.
6 Altamira, R., *A History of Spain*, New York, 1949, p 118.
7 An interesting account will be found in T. D. Kendrick, *St James in Spain*, London, 1960.

3 THE GOLDEN AGE

8 Granada, Luis de, *Historia de Sor María y Sermón de las Caídas Públicas*, Barcelona, 1962, p 386.
9 Trevor Davies, R., *The Golden Century of Spain*, London, 1964, p 13.
10 Quoted in M. Bataillon's *Prólogo* to the *Enquiridion*, Madrid, 1932, p 49.
11 Elliott, J. H., *Imperial Spain, 1469–1716*, London, 1963, p 13.
12 *Ibid.*, p 108.
13 *Ibid.*, p 102.
14 The reference is to Amadis of Gaul, the most popular of the romances of chivalry. See Bernal Diaz: *The Conquest of New Spain*, tr. by J. M. Cohen, Penguin Books, 1963, p 214.
15 Quoted by M. Defourneaux in *La Vie Quotidienne en Espagne au Siècle d'Or*, Paris, 1964, p 168.
16 He is generally referred to as Charles *V*, since he was the fifth Emperor of that name, though he was also King Charles *I* of Spain.

17 Quoted by Trevor Davies, *op. cit.*, p 47.

18 Elliott, *op. cit.*, p 150.

19 Hanke, L., *Aristotle and the American Indians*, London, 1959, p 107.

20 The *Autobiography* or Testament of St Ignatius Loyola, Chapter 1.

21 Interesting records of this nature continue to come to light. One fascinating example is the spiritual autobiography of María Vela, a nun of Avila and younger contemporary of Saint Teresa, whose raptures caused a great stir in their day. An English version by F. Parkinson Keyes has been published under the title of *The Third Mystic*, London, 1960.

22 San Juan de la Cruz's poetry can be read in the fine translation by R. Campbell, Penguin Books, 1960.

23 Brenan, G., *The Literature of the Spanish People*, Cambridge, 1951, p 156.

24 For an illuminating study see A. A. Parker: *Literature and the Delinquent: the Picaresque Novel in Spain and Europe*, Edinburgh, 1967.

25 John Osborne has turned one of Lope's plays to horrific effect in his *A Bond Honoured*. For a stimulating insight into the 'honour' theme see A. A. Parker: *The Approach to the Spanish Drama of the Golden Age*, Diamante Booklet, 1957, and for a full treatment of the Spanish theatre see the monumental work by N. D. Shergold: *A History of the Spanish Stage*, Oxford, 1967.

26 His poetry can be read, with its Latinized word-order straightened out, in the verse translation by E. M. Wilson: *The Solitudes of Don Luis de Góngora*, Cambridge, 1931.

27 Brenan, *op. cit.*, p 243.

4 THE AFTERMATH OF EMPIRE

28 Madariaga, S. de, *Spain*, London, 1946, p 62.

29 Orwell, G.; *Homage to Catalonia*, London, 1938, pp 2–3.

30 The Nationalists declared that it was the 'Reds' who destroyed Guernica. (See Bolín's *Spain: The Vital Years* pp 335–60 for a recent account of this version.) The evidence of journalists who visited the bombed city, as given in Steer's *The Tree of Gernika*, London, 1938, and of the German officers at the Nuremberg trials makes a very different story. Crozier finds it difficult to assign 'the proportionate degree of responsibility', but is inclined to put most of the blame on the Republicans.

5 FRANCO'S SPAIN – THE POLITICAL AND ECONOMIC SCENE

31 Julio Busquets Bragulat: *El Militar de Carrera en España*, Barcelona, 1967. Another observer, however, regards the officer corps as a largely self-perpetuating élite: 'during the three years 1961–3 approximately 70 per cent

of the new officer candidates were sons of army men; of these about $\frac{2}{3}$ were offspring of officers and approximately $\frac{1}{3}$ sons of NCOs and enlisted men'. Stanley G. Payne: *Politics and the Military in Modern Spain*, Stanford University Press, 1967, p 447.

32 Quoted by Gerald Brenan: *The Spanish Labyrinth*, Cambridge, 1943, p 130.

33 J. Anlló: *Estructura y Problemas del Campo Español*, Madrid, 1967, p 37. It should not, however, be assumed that all members of the great landed aristocracy are without social conscience. Some have been noted for their radical spirit. The sixteenth Duke of Medina Sidonia was one of the first of the grandees to renounce his feudal privileges at the beginning of the nineteenth century. The mother of the present Duchess turned the family palace into a clinic, and the present Duchess has championed many left-wing causes.

34 Whitaker, A. P., *Spain and the Defense of the West*, New York, 1961, p 220.

35 R. Tamames: *Cuatro Problemas de la Economía Española*, Madrid, 1965, pp 172–4.

36 Tamames, R., *Estructura Económica de España*, Madrid, 1960, pp 51–2.

37 Anlló: *op. cit.*, p 31.

38 Madariaga, *op. cit.*, p 149.

39 Quoted by Peers: *Catalonia Infelix*, London, 1937, p 180.

40 Ambrosio Zatarain in *Cuadernos para el Diálogo*, October, 1966.

6 TRADITIONAL ATTITUDES AND NEW TRENDS

41 Brenan, *The Spanish Labyrinth*, pp 47–8.

42 Kenny, M., *Spanish Tapestry; town and country in Castile*, London, 1961, pp 146–7.

43 Welles, B., *Spain: the Gentle Anarchy*, London, 1965, pp 154–167.

44 M. del Jesús and A. Ramiro, *Santos Españoles*, Madrid, 15th edition, 1939, with a foreword by the Bishop of Madrid-Alcalá, p 10.

45 Interesting examples of this cult will be found in C. Lison Tolosana: *Belmonte de los Caballeros*, Oxford, 1966.

46 R. Duocastella *et al.*, *Análisis Sociológico del Catolicismo Español*, Barcelona, 1967, pp 54 and 112.

47 *Ibid.*, p 74.

48 Mary Salas, in *Cuadernos para el Diálogo*, the most interesting independent journal now published in Spain, in a special issue of December 1965 devoted to the present status of women.

49 René Pelissier: 'Spain's Discreet Decolonization' in *Foreign Affairs*, April 1965, p 519.

50 José María Doussinague: *España tenía Razón*, Madrid, 1949.

51 H. Feis, *The Spanish Story: Franco and the Nations at War*, 1948, p 8.

52 See the United States official publication *The Spanish Government and the Axis*, Washington, 1946, which reproduces numerous documents from captured Axis archives, and the official Spanish reply: *Réplica a la publicación .. de documentos relativos a España*, Madrid, 1946.

53 *The Spanish Economy in 1966*, prepared by the Banco Urquidi, pp 64–8.

54 See Tamames, R., 'España y la Integración Europea' in *Cuatro Problemas de la Economía Española*.

55 Spanish newspapers now sometimes carry advertisements by Spanish Republican exiles long resident in the Soviet Union offering their services as commercial representatives for firms in Franco's Spain wishing to do business with the Russians.

Select Bibliography

NOTE   This list is limited to works in English

GENERAL

Allison-Peers, E., *Spain: A Companion to Spanish Studies*, London, 1929
  Catalonia Infelix, London, 1937
Altamira, R., *A History of Spain*, New York, 1949
Borrow, George, *The Bible in Spain*, London, 1842, and various editions
Brenan, Gerald, *The Spanish Labyrinth*, Cambridge, 1943, and paperback
  The Literature of the Spanish People, Cambridge, 1951, and paperback
Fitzmaurice-Kelly, J. A., *A New History of Spanish Literature*, Oxford, 1926
Ford, Richard, *Handbook for Travellers in Spain*, London, 1845; repr. 1966
  Gatherings from Spain, London, 1846, and Everyman's edition
Ganivet, Angel, *Spain: an Interpretation*, London, 1946 (English version of
  the *Idearium Español*)
Langdon Davies, J., *Gatherings from Catalonia*, London, 1953
Madariaga, Salvador de, *Spain*, London, 1942
  The Genius of Spain, Oxford, 1923
Ortega y Gasset, J., *Invertebrate Spain*, London, 1937
Oliveira Martins, J. P., *A History of Iberian Civilization*, Oxford, 1930
Pritchett, V. S., *The Spanish Temper*, London, 1954
Trend, J. B., *Civilizations of Spain*, Oxford, 1944; new ed. 1968
Trueta, J., *The Spirit of Catalonia*, Oxford, 1946

ROMAN, MEDIEVAL, AND ISLAMIC SPAIN

Castro, A., *The Structure of Spanish History*, Princeton, 1954
Clissold, S., *In Search of the Cid*, London, 1965
Hole, E., *Andalus – Spain under the Moslems*, London, 1958
Menéndez Pidal, R., *The Cid and his Spain*, London, 1934; new ed. 1968
Merwin, W. S., *The Poem of the Cid*, London, 1959

Montgomery Watt, *History of Islamic Spain*, Edinburgh, 1965
Sutherland, C. H. V., *The Romans in Spain*, London, 1939

THE GOLDEN AGE

Allison-Peers, E., *Spanish Mysticism*, London, 1924
Bell, Aubrey, *Luis de León*, Oxford, 1925
Elliott, J. H., *Imperial Spain, 1469–1716*, London, 1963
Hanke, Lewis, *Aristotle and the American Indians*, London, 1959
Kamen, H., *The Spanish Inquisition*, London, 1965
Kirkpatrick, F. A., *The Spanish Conquistadores*, London, 1934
Klein, J., *The Mesta: a study in Spanish economic history*, Cambridge, Mass., 1920
Lea, C. H., *A History of the Inquisition*, 4 vols, New York, 1918–34
Merriman, R. B., *The Rise of the Spanish Empire in the Old World and the New*, 4 vols., New York, 1918–22
Mattingly, Garrett, *The Defeat of the Spanish Armada*, London, 1959
Prescott, W. H., *History of the Reign of Ferdinand and Isabella the Catholic*, 3 vols., London, 1838
   History of the Reign of Philip II, London, 1878
Trevor Davies, R., *The Golden Century of Spain*, London, 1937 and paperback
Seaver, H. J., *The Great Revolt in Castille*, London, 1928
Walsh, W. T., *Philip II*, London, 1938

THE AFTERMATH OF EMPIRE

Carr, Raymond, *Spain, 1808–1939*, Oxford, 1966
Hamilton, E. J., *War and Prices in Spain, 1651–1800*, Cambridge, Mass., 1947
Hennessy, C. A. M., *The Federal Republic in Spain*, Oxford, 1962
Herr, R., *The Eighteenth Century Revolution in Spain*, Princeton University Press, 1958
Holt, E., *The Carlist Wars in Spain*, London, 1967
Madariaga, S. de, *The Fall of the Spanish Empire*, London, 1947
Oman, Charles, *A History of the Peninsular War*, 7 vols, Oxford, 1912–30
Ramos Oliveira, A., *Politics, Economics, and Men of Modern Spain*, London, 1946
Robertson, W. S., *Rise of the Latin American Republics*, New York and London, 1918
Trend, J. B., *The Origins of Modern Spain*, Cambridge, 1934

REPUBLIC AND CIVIL WAR

Bolín, L., *Spain: the Vital Years*, London, 1967

Bolloten, B., *The Grand Camouflage*, London, 1961

Borkenau, G., *The Spanish Cockpit*, London, 1937, and paperback

Buckley, H., *Life and Death of the Spanish Republic*, London, 1940

Jackson, G., *The Spanish Republic and the Civil War*, Princeton University Press, 1965, and paperback

Orwell, George, *Homage to Catalonia*, London, 1938

Payne, R., *The Civil War in Spain*, London, 1962

Payne, S., *Falange*, Oxford, 1962

Payne, S., *Politics and the Military in Modern Spain*, Stanford University Press, 1967

Puzzo, Dante A., *Spain and the Great Powers, 1936–41*, New York, 1962

Thomas, Hugh, *The Spanish Civil War*, London, 1961, and paperback

Sanchez, J. M., *Reform and Reaction: the politico-religious background of the Spanish Civil War*, North Carolina, 1964

Steer, G. L., *The Tree of Gernika*, London, 1938

FRANCO'S SPAIN

Crozier, Brian, *Franco: a biographical history*, London, 1967

Hills, George, *Franco: the Man and his Nation*, London, 1967

Payne, S., *Franco's Spain*, New York and London, 1967, and paperback

Szulc, Tad, *The Bombs of Palomares*, London, 1967

Welles, B., *Spain: the Gentle Anarchy*, London, 1965

Whitaker, A. P., *Spain and Defense of the West*, New York, 1961, and paperback

Acknowledgements

Anne Bolt, 2, 23, 28, 30, 32, 35; British Museum, 8; Camera Press, 6, 18, 19, 31, 33; Foto Mas, Barcelona, 9, 12, 13, 21, 24, 34; John R. Freeman, 3; M. Hürlimann, 4, 25; Keystone Press Agency, 20; MAS, 10, 15; Ministerio de Información y Turismo, 7, 22, 26, 27; Museo del Prado, 16; Museum of Modern Art, New York, 17; National Gallery, London; 11; Photographie Giraudon, 14; Radio Times, 5; Spanish National Tourist Office, 1, 29.

The maps on page 113 are adapted from Raymond Carr, *Spain 1809–1939* (Clarendon Press, Oxford).

Who's Who

ALMANZOR (Ibn Abī Amir, known as Al-Mansūr, 'the Victorious') (d. 1002). Rose in the Caliph of Cordova's service to be Commander-in-Chief and all-powerful minister. Celebrated for his ruthlessness, fanaticism, and his destructive campaigns against the Christians.

AZAÑA, MANUEL (1880–1940). Civil servant of upright but rigid character who, as Prime Minister in the Second Republic, attempted to carry out a series of radical reforms. In 1936 he exchanged the premiership for the presidency and later withdrew from politics.

BAROJA, PÍO (1872–1956). Prolific novelist of Basque origin. His work shows the influence of Dickens, Balzac, and the picaresque tradition and is noted for its realism, pessimism, dry humour, anti-clericalism and verve.

BORBÓN Y BATTENBERG, Don Juan, Count of Barcelona (b. 1913). Third son of the late Alfonso XIII and Pretender to the Spanish throne, living in Portugal. Has served with the Spanish and British navies and is a keen yachtsman. Reputed to be of liberal sympathies, he has expressed some criticism of Franco's régime, but is permitted to make occasional visits to Spain.

BORBÓN Y BORBÓN, Don Juan Carlos (b. 1938). Son of the Pretender Don Juan. Educated in Spain by agreement with Franco. His succession to the throne is reputedly favoured in some quarters in preference to that of his father.

CALDERÓN DE LA BARCA, PEDRO (1600–81). The last great dramatist of Spain's Golden Age. Many of his plays deal with the theme of 'honour'. His finest, such as *Life is a Dream*, are notable for their religious and philosophical inspiration and for the baroque magnificence of their verse.

CALVO SOTELO, JOSÉ (1893–1936). Minister of Finance under Primo de Rivera and right-wing political leader. His assassination precipitated the Civil War.

CAMBÓ, FRANCISCO DE ASÍS (1876–1947). Catalan industrialist, lawyer, and nationalist leader; the political heir to Prat de la Riba (Q.V.)

CÁNOVAS DEL CASTILLO, ANTONIO (1828–97). Malagan journalist, politician, and historian. The leading conservative statesman in the Restoration period following the First Republic.

CARRERO BLANCO, Vice-Admiral Luis (b. 1903). Vice-President of the Government and a personal friend of Franco. Following his career in the navy, he became secretary of the Cabinet Council. Author of various books on naval and military history. Regarded as one of the most inflexibly right-wing members of the government.

CASTIELLA, FERNANDO MARÍA (b. 1907). Foreign Minister in the Franco government. Of Basque origin, he came to Franco's attention as the author of a book setting out Spain's claims to large parts of France's African empire and to the return of Gibraltar; the latter remains an objective of his foreign policy. Volunteered in 1942 for service with the Blue Division against Russia. Founder and first director of the Falangist-inspired Institute for Political Studies. Ambassador to the Vatican, where he negotiated the 1953 Concordat. Since his appointment as Foreign Minister in 1957 he has worked for closer relations with West Europe and for the improvement of Spain's image by ending discrimination against Protestants.

CELA, CAMILO JOSÉ (b. 1916). Author of novels in the picaresque tradition and of descriptions of travel through backward parts of Spain. His best-known books are *Pascual Duarte's Family* (1942) and *The Bee-Hive* (1951), a vast panorama of Madrid life.

CERVANTES, MIGUEL DE (1547–1616). Spain's most famous writer. Served as a soldier and was wounded at Lepanto; later spent five years as prisoner of the Moors. On returning to Spain, he made a precarious living whilst writing unsuccessful plays, a pastoral novel, and the excellent *Exemplary Novels* (short stories). The publication of *Don Quixote* (1605) marked him as Spain's greatest literary genius.

CHARLES (CARLOS) V, Emperor (Charles I, King of Spain) (1500–58). The first of Spain's Hapsburg dynasty, who spent much of his reign defending his imperial interests against France, the Turks, the Papacy, and the Protestant princes. He abdicated in 1556 and died in retirement at the monastery of Yuste (Estremadura).

CISNEROS, Cardinal (also known as Ximénez de Cisneros) (1436–1517). Appointed, whilst a Franciscan friar, to be confessor to Queen Isabel. His prudent counsels, strength of character, and zeal to reform Church abuses raised him to be Archbishop of Toledo and Metropolitan, and he was twice Regent of Spain. He was also a great patron of learning and renowned for his upright, ascetic life.

COMPANYS, LUIS (1883–1940). Catalan lawyer and politician. Headed the autonomous Catalan government (Generalitat) after the collapse of the monarchy (1931). Executed by the Nationalists for his part in the Civil War.

CORTÉS, HERNÁN (1485–1547). The son of a family of modest Estremaduran nobles. He led a small expedition to Mexico and succeeded in overthrowing the Aztec empire. The Crown confirmed him as Governor of 'New Spain', but on his return to Europe gave him no further scope for his ambitions and talents.

DÍAZ DE VIVAR, RODRIGO (known as the Cid) (d. 1099). Famous for his military prowess and hero of the oldest Spanish epic and of numerous ballads and plays. Exiled from Castile by Alfonso VI, he carved out a principality for himself at Valencia and was the only Christian general capable of defeating the Almoravides.

EL GRECO (Domenikos Theotocopulos) (1541–1614). Of Greek origin and trained in Italy, he settled in Toledo where he painted portraits and religious pictures. His work is strikingly original in its range of colour, elongation of human forms, and the blending of human and divine elements in one grandiose conception (e.g. *Burial of Count Orgaz*).

ESCRIVÁ DE BALAGUER Y ALBÁS, JOSÉ MARÍA (b. 1902). Founder and President General of *Opus Dei*. Now resident in Rome. His book *Camino* is reported to have sold more than a million copies.

FALLA, MANUEL DE (1876–1946). Best known of modern Spanish composers. His work shows much French influence, but draws liberally on colourful Andalusian folk motifs.

FERDINAND of Aragon ('The Catholic'; 1452–1516). Husband of Isabel of Castile. Noted for his political astuteness, he was the model for Machiavelli's *The Prince*.

FERDINAND III, King of Castile, Saint (1217–52). Famous for his pious and upright character and for his military prowess. He captured Seville from the Moors in 1248 and was canonized after his death.

FRAGA IRIBARNE, MANUEL (b. 1922). Minister of Information and Tourism since 1962. Previously a Professor of Law, he is the author of some 30 books on the press, art, constitutional and social subjects. He is regarded as one of the more liberal of Franco's ministers.

FRANCO Y BAHAMONDE, Generalissimo FRANCISCO (b. 1892). The undisputed master of Spain since the end of the Civil War. He was born at Ferrol, Galicia, and had military training in Morocco. At the age of 34 he was made a general and then served five years as director of the Military Academy at Saragossa. Appointed Commander-in-Chief, Morocco, in 1934, he was summoned to suppress the rising of the Asturian miners, then relegated, as a potential danger to the Republic, to be Captain-General in the Canaries. After conspiring with other army leaders, he issued a manifesto against the government on 18 July 1936 and flew to Morocco to assume command of the rising there. He was proclaimed Caudillo of the Nationalist forces on 1 October 1936.

GANIVET, ANGEL (1865–98). Essayist and novelist notable for his interpretations of Spanish history and character, *Idearium Español* and *The Future of Spain*.

GARCÍA LORCA, FEDERICO (1899–1936). Andalusian poet and dramatist murdered at the outbreak of the Civil War. His most popular work is probably his *Romancero Gitano*, a stylized evocation of the gypsy world in traditional ballad form.

GARCILASO DE LA VEGA (1503–36). Courtier, soldier, and poet. Revivified Spanish poetry through his fresh lyrical inspiration and by his skilful adaptation of classical and Italian forms.

GIL ROBLES, JOSÉ MARÍA (b. 1898). Leader of the Christian Democrats under the Second Republic. Now represents the moderate right-wing Catholic monarchist line in opposition to the present régime.

GIMÉNEZ FERNÁNDEZ, Professor MANUEL (b. 1896). Professor of Canon Law at Seville University and leader of a left-wing Christian Democrat Party. Was Minister of Agriculture in the Second Republic and author of its land reform law.

GINER DE LOS RÍOS, FRANCISCO (1839–1915). Outstanding education-alist and founder of the Institución Libre de Enseñanza which influenced many of Spain's liberal writers and thinkers.

GÓNGORA, LUIS DE (1561–1627). Foremost poet of the later Golden Age. After composing many excellent lyrics, sonnets, and ballads, he evolved the complex, baroque, heavily latinized style known as *culteranismo*. His major work, *The Solitudes*, is written in this style.

GOYA, FRANCISCO DE (1746–1828). Spain's greatest eighteenth-century painter, remarkable for the force and variety of his work, which ranges from court and society portraits to scenes of popular life and moving episodes of war and macabre fantasy.

GOYTISOLO, JUAN (b. 1931). One of the most forceful and talented of the younger writers, whose novels depict the corruption and futility of contemporary society.

GRANADA, LUIS DE (1506–88). Dominican monk, preacher, and author of numerous mystical and devotional prose-works.

ISABEL, Queen of Castile ('The Catholic') (1451–1504). Her marriage to Ferdinand of Aragon linked that kingdom to Castile and laid the foundation for Spain's greatness. Under their rule the Reconquest was completed, Columbus discovered America, the Jews were expelled from Spain, and many reforms of state and church carried out.

ISIDORE, St (circa 560–636). Archbishop of Seville in succession to his brother, St Leander. Composed a *History of the Goths*, the encyclopaedic *Etymologies* and other works. Famous for his learning, sanctity, organizing abilities, and cham-pionship of the Catholic Church against Arianism.

JAMES (JAIME) 1, King of Aragon ('The Conqueror') (1208–76). Conquered Majorca (1229) and Valencia (1238) from the Moslems.

JIMÉNEZ, JUAN RAMÓN (1881–1958). Andalusian writer and probably the major figure in Spanish poetry of this century. Following the Civil War he lived in exile in the United States. His *Platero y Yo*, a favourite with children, is a masterpiece of poetic prose.

JOHN of Austria, Don (1545–78). Natural son of Charles V and half-brother to Philip II. Commanded the Spanish forces at the victory of Lepanto.

JOHN of the Cross, St (1542–91). Monk and poet, associated with St Teresa in the reform of the Carmelite Order. His poems are the supreme expression of Spanish mystical literature.

LAÍN ENTRALGO, PEDRO (b. 1908). Professor of the History of Medicine and Rector of Madrid University until resigning after differences with the régime. Author of several books on medical subjects (e.g. *Mind and Body*, London, 1955) and politics (*España como problema*, 1956).

LARGO CABALLERO, FRANCISCO (1869–1946). Leader of the Socialist Trade Unions. Headed the Republican Government during the Civil War between Sept. 1936 and May 1937.

LEÓN, LUIS DE (1527–91). Augustinian monk and professor at Salamanca University. Author of prose works and poems of mystical, platonic, and classical inspiration.

LÓPEZ BRAVO, GREGORIO (b. 1923). Minister of Industry since 1962. Formerly Director of Foreign Exchange Institute.

LÓPEZ RODÓ, LAUREANO (b. 1920). Commissioner for the government's Development Plan since 1962, and Minister without Portfolio. Professor of Administrative Law at Santiago University (1945–53). Prominent member of *Opus Dei*.

LOYOLA, IGNATIUS, St (d. 1556). Born of a Basque noble family, he served as a soldier. Whilst recovering from wounds, conceived a vocation for the religious life. Founder of the Society of Jesus as a body of dedicated men to serve the Pope. His *Spiritual Exercises* is their training manual. He directed the new Jesuit Order from Rome until his death.

LULL (LLULL, LULIO), RAMÓN (d. 1315). Majorcan mystic, philosopher, and missionary. Devoted his life to composition of works designed to prove the mysteries of the Christian faith by reason and so achieve the peaceful conversion of Jews and Moslems. His tireless travels and missionary activities culminated in his martyrdom in North Africa.

MACHADO, ANTONIO (1875-1939). Though of Andalusian origin, he spent much of his life working as a schoolmaster in Castile, and his poetry is mostly concerned with Castilian landscapes and themes. His brother Manuel, also a fine poet, remained more Andalusian in inspiration.

MADARIAGA, SALVADOR DE (b. 1886). Writer, historian, and liberal politician living in exile. Under the Second Republic he was Minister of Education and Delegate to the League of Nations. He has held appointments at Oxford and other universities and is the author of numerous works of history, biography, literary criticism, and fiction.

MAEZTU Y WHITNEY, RAMIRO (1874-1936). Writer, journalist, and diplomat. Of mixed Basque and British parentage, he changed from a left-wing to an ultra-conservative position and was murdered during the Civil War. His *Defensa de la Hispanidad* is an extreme Catholic exegesis of Spanish civilization with emphasis on the cultural unity of the Spanish-speaking nations.

MARAÑÓN, GREGORIO (1887-1960). Historian, essayist, and endocrynologist. His biographies (e.g. of Antonio Pérez, Feijoo, Enrique IV of Castile) and his essays on the Don Juan myth, where historical interpretation is illumined by medical insight, are particularly valuable.

MAURA, ANTONIO (1853-1925). Majorcan lawyer and Conservative statesman. Attempted, with little success, to make Spain's parliamentary system effective and to settle the Catalan question.

MENÉNDEZ Y PELAYO, MARCELINO (1856-1912). Literary critic and historian of vast output and strong Catholic views. Wrote monumental works on Spanish aesthetics, heterodoxy, science, and poetry.

MENÉNDEZ PIDAL, RAMÓN (b. 1869). Doyen of Spanish scholars. Has carried out important historical, philological, and literary research, particularly relating to medieval Spain.

MIRÓ, JOAN (b. 1893). Catalan painter, now mainly resident in Paris, with a world reputation for his paintings, sculpture, engravings, and ceramics.

MOLINA, TIRSO DE (d. 1648). Pen-name of Friar Gabriel Téllez, author of numerous plays, and creator, in his *El Burlador de Sevilla*, of Don Juan.

MUÑOZ GRANDES, AGUSTÍN (b. 1896). Old comrade-in-arms of Franco, former commander of the Blue Division, and for a short time Secretary General of the Falange. As Captain-General (1957) and Vice-Premier (1962), he has been one of the most influential figures in the army and government.

NEGRÍN, Dr JUAN (1889–1956). Madrid University Professor and Socialist politician. Headed the last Popular Front government of the Second Republic (May 1937–9).

OLIVARES, GASPAR DE GUZMÁN, Count-Duke (1587–1645). All-powerful minister of Philip IV. Attempted to restore Spain's greatness by ambitious projects and reforms.

ORTEGA Y GASSET, JOSÉ (1883–1955). Essayist and journalist. After education in Germany, he became Professor of Metaphysics at Madrid and founded the influential *Revista de Occidente*. His *Invertebrate Spain* is a penetrating analysis of Spain's decadence, and his *Revolt of the Masses* (against the élite who created its civilization) an analysis of the ills of Western Europe.

PÉREZ GALDÓS, BENITO (1843–1920). Prolific Spanish novelist, whose *Episodios Nacionales* (46 volumes) and other series of novels are comparable in scope to Balzac's *Comédie Humaine*.

PHILIP II, King of Spain (1527–98). Succeeded his father Charles V as King of Spain in 1556. Devoted himself to the defence of the Catholic faith, which he identified with Spanish national interests, against Protestants and Turks. He has been censured for the coldness, fanaticism, and duplicity of his character, but he was also conscientious, hard-working, and a patron of the arts.

PI Y MARGALL, FRANCISCO (1824-1901). Catalan intellectual and federal theorist. President of the short-lived First Republic (1873).

PICASSO, PABLO RUIZ (b. 1881). Educated in Barcelona and mainly resident, since 1901, in France. Founder and leader of the Cubist school. Now universally recognized as one of the greatest living creative artists.

PIZARRO, FRANCISCO (1475-1541). Reputed to have started life as a swineherd in Estremadura, he sought his fortune in the New World and discovered and conquered the Inca empire. A daring leader of men, he lacked the qualities of a statesman and was assassinated at the hands of a hostile faction.

PRAT DE LA RIBA, ENRICH (1870-1917). Organizer and leading intellectual exponent of Catalan nationalism, and advocate of a federal constitution for Spain.

PRIMO DE RIVERA, JOSÉ ANTONIO (1903-36). Son of General Primo de Rivera and founder of the Falange. Murdered at the onset of the Civil War.

PRIMO DE RIVERA, General MIGUEL (1870-1936). Seized power in 1923 to reestablish 'social peace', purge the politicians, and bring the war in Morocco to an end. He ruled Spain in autocratic but paternalistic fashion until the economic crisis led to his fall and exile in 1929.

QUEVEDO, FRANCISCO DE (d. 1645). Author of poems, novels (*El Buscón*), fantasies (*Los Sueños*), and other varied works, generally satirical or burlesque in tone.

RAMÓN Y CAJAL, SANTIAGO (1852-1934). Spain's leading scientist, whose work laid the foundation of modern neurology.

RIDRUEJO, DIONISIO (b. 1912). Poet and former Falangist propagandist. Broke with the régime and founded his small Partido Social de Acción Democrática.

RUIZ GIMÉNEZ, Dr JOAQUÍN (b. 1912). Liberal Catholic leader. Formerly Ambassador to the Holy See, Director of Instituto de Cultura Hispánica and Minister of Education.

SOLÍS RUIZ, JOSÉ (b. 1913). Andalusian lawyer, Secretary General of the Falange and head of the *sindicatos*, with rank of Minister.

TERESA of Avila, St (1515-82). After a number of years in a Carmelite convent at Avila, she conceived a vocation to work for the reform of that Order, and despite violent opposition, succeeded in founding a number of houses where the stricter primitive rule of the 'discalced Carmelites' could be observed. In her practice of mental prayer she experienced frequent ecstasies and revelations which are known to us through her *Life*, written at the request of her Confessor, and in the devotional works composed for the guidance of her nuns. Her warm, vivid personality, practical yet visionary, marks her as one of the most remarkable of Spanish women.

ULLASTRES CALVO, Dr ALBERTO (b. 1914). Ambassador to the EEC since 1965. Formerly Minister of Commerce and Professor of Political Economy and Finance, Madrid University. Member of *Opus Dei*.

UNAMUNO, MIGUEL DE (1864-1936). Outstanding writer and thinker of Basque origin. Spent much of his life as Professor of Greek and Rector of Salamanca University. In such works as *The Life of Don Quixote and Sancho Panza* and *The Tragic Sense of Life* he shows a passionate concern for the problems of Spain, the dilemma of reconciling faith and human knowledge, and man's obsessive desire for individual survival.

VALLE INCLÁN, RAMÓN MARÍA DEL (1869-1936). Novelist, poet, and dramatist of Galician origin. One of the most colourful and original figures of the 'Generation of Ninety-Eight.'

VEGA, LOPE DE (1562-1635). The most prolific and inventive writer of Spain's Golden Age, and the creator of the Spanish three-act *comedia*, of which some 500 examples from his pen survive. He also wrote a novel, *La Dorotea*, and many admirable lyrics. His adventurous life included service with the Invincible Armada.

VELÁSQUEZ, DIEGO DE (1599-1660). Close companion to Philip IV and remained in his service for nearly 40 years. He excelled as a portrait painter, and also painted larger compositions like the *Surrender of Breda* and *Las Meninas* which rank him as one of Spain's greatest artists.

Index

Cortes, 53, 70, 95, 110, 120, 126–7, 150, 159
Cortés, Hernán (*see* Who's Who, p. 197), 24, 51, 66
Corunna (La Coruña), 15, 132, 146
Costa, Joaquín, 105
Costa Brava, 19–20
Cuba, 8, 100, 104–5, 183–6

DALI, SALVADOR, 160
Díaz del Castillo, Bernal, 57, 67
Dominic, St, 60
Don Alfonso (Borbón), 123
Don Carlos, 74
Don Hugo Carlos (de Bourbon Parma), 123
Don Juan (Borbón y Battenberg) (*see* Who's Who, p. 195), 123, 151, 186
Don Juan Carlos (Borbón y Borbón) (*see* Who's Who, p. 195), 123, 151, 186, *19*
Don Juan Tenorio, 81
Don Juan of Austria (*see* Who's Who, p. 200), 72, 74
Duero, River, 25, 48

EBRO, RIVER 17, 102, 117
Economic conditions, 28, 63–6, 94–6, 107, 127–34, 178–9
Education, 104, 134, 154–5
Elche, 11, 21, 32
El Cordobés, 160
El Empecinado, 99
El Ferrol, 15
El Greco (*see* Who's Who, p. 197), 25, 75–6
Emigration, 15, 23, 28–9, 140–2
Emporion, 18, 32
Enlightenment, The, 96–7, 99, 101
Enrique IV, 54
Erasmus, 62–3
Escurial (El Escorial), 75
Escrivá, José Maria (*see* Who's Who, p. 197), 150
Estremadura (Extremadura), 23–4, 28, 64
Euzkadi (*see* also under Basque), 145
Exports, 135, 179–80, 183–4

FALANGE, 110–11, 119, 121–4, 130–2, 147, 151, 158
Falla, Manuel de (*see* Who's Who, p. 198)
Feijoo, Benito Jerónimo, 96
Ferdinand (Fernando) I, 48
Ferdinand III ('The Saint'), (*see* Who's Who, p. 198), 40, 51
Ferdinand V of Castile, II of Aragon (*see* Who's Who, p. 198), 16, 18, 40, 54–6, 68
Ferdinand VII, 98–102
Ferdinand of Antequera, 52
Floridablanca, 96
Ford, Richard, 7, 21, 26
Fraga Iribarne, Manuel (*see* Who's Who, p. 198)
Franco, General Francisco (*see* Who's Who, p. 198), 15, 110–18, 119–86 *passim, 18*

GALICIA, 14–15, 28, 31, 48–9, 136, 138, 141, 143, 145–6, 149
Ganivet, Angel (*see* Who's Who, p. 198), 26, 93, 105
García Lorca, Federico, (*see* Who's Who, p. 198), 160
Garcilaso de la Vega (*see* Who's Who, p. 198), 79
Gaudí, Antonio, 30, *34*
'Generation of '98', 104–6
Gerona, 18, 34
Gibraltar, 36, 93, 174, 176, 180–1, 183
Gil Robles, José María (*see* Who's Who, p. 199), 110, 124
Giner de los Ríos, Francisco (*see* Who's Who, p. 199), 104
Ginés de Sepúlveda, Juan, 71
Godoy, Manuel, 97–8
Góngora, Luis de (*see* Who's Who, p. 199), 82
González, Fernán, 48
Goya, Francisco (*see* Who's Who, p. 199), 97
Goytisolo, Juan (*see* Who's Who, p. 199), 161–2

Servet, Miguel, 162
Seville (Sevilla), 11, 22, 34, 43, 45, 51, 63–5, 94–5, 99, 114, 132, 182
Sierra Morena, 22, 96
Sierra Nevada, 22, 59
Socialists, 106, 110–11, 115, 124–5, 147
Solís, José (see Who's Who, p. 204), 130
Soria, 141
Soviet Union, 176–7, 182–3
Spanish Guinea, 173
Suanzes, Juan Antonio, 129

TAGUS (Tajo), river, 24–5, 114
Taifas, 39, 41
Talavera, 54
Talavera, Hernán de, 59
Talayots, 31
Tarragona, 18, 34, *2*
Teresa de Avila, St (see Who's Who, p. 204), 25, 67, 78, 83, 158
Teruel, 18, 117
Textiles, 19
Tirso de Molina (see Who's Who, p. 202), 81
Toledo, 25, 34, 35, 59–60, 75–6, 79, 114–15, 136, *24*
Torres Villaroel, Diego de, 97
Tourism, 128, 132, 178
Trade, 65, 95, 133
Trade Unions, 106, 120, 129–30, 148, 155
Trajan, 33, 127

ULLASTRES CALVO, ALBERTO (see Who's Who, p. 204), 131, 150
Umar Ibn Hafsūn, 38
Unamuno, Miguel de (see Who's Who, p. 204), 17, 46, 106
United Nations, 177–81
United States of America, 8, 104, 122, 178–84, 186
Universities, 62, 79, 151, 154–5, 159
Utrecht, Treaty of, 180

VALENCIA, 11, 20–1, 57–8, 69
Valladolid, 24, 63, 71, 132
Valle Inclán, Ramón María del (see Who's Who, p. 204), 105, 163
Vega, Lope de (see Who's Who, p. 204), 80–1, *10*
Velásquez (see Who's Who, p. 204), 76
Vigo, 15, 132, 146
Villalar, 69
Visigoths, 32–6, 47–8
Vitoria, 154

WELLINGTON, Duke of, 7, 97, 99
Witiza, King, 36
Women, status of, 157–9
Workers Commissions, 152

YAGÜE, Colonel, 114

ZORILLA, JOSÉ, 81
Zurbarán, Francisco, 77, *12*